# FAST BREAK

Creating A Customer-Centric
Operating Philosophy
for Automotive Service

By Jim Roche

# Dedication

For my family and friends—thanks for always believing.

# Acknowledgements

Once again, huge thank you to Lance Helgeson, whose insight, wit, guiding hand and writing skill make these projects as good as they can be and a lot of fun.

And thank you to Dale Buss for getting us rolling and then adding some polish.

Thank you to those who contributed to the content of this book. These great service leaders: Billy Monteverde, Lee Bradley, Todd Ruprecht, Jim Woodall, Trevor Gile, Tully Williams, Vince Sweeney,

Robert Scott, Marno Muth, Dawn Newsome, Donnie Pelkey, Jack Turske, Chris Ward, Ramzy Handal, Scott Witt, Christopher Ouellette, Steve Nicholson, along with these great automotive professionals: Mir Baqar, Darrel Ferguson, Claire Pillarelli, Nicole Redding, Gregg Manson, Jim Coleman, Kevin Filan, David Foutz, Matt Bateman, Candy Lucey, Brady McFadden, Marisa Molenda and the Farm team, Lisa Aloisio, Angela Drake, Sonia Kher, Amy Anderson, Joe Skehan, Bobby Chen, Ivan Cuevas Ortin, Meng Liu and thanks again to Dale Pollak for lighting the road ahead with Velocity.

And those who helped produce it: Philana Chiu, Stephanie Dang, Karuna Koy, Angel Trinh, Steve Chandless, Brenda Berg, Terri Shackleford, Stacy Rager, Jason Earle, Greg Criss, Jon Q.

Great cover design - Jamie Tan and Ariana Brogan, with Chris Lozada, Darrell Noe, and Lesley Starks

If I've overlooked anyone – thank you for your help!

My appreciation to Cheryl, Kayleigh, Marissa and Davis.

# 2020 Acknowledgements

As always, Lance Helgeson asks the thought-provoking questions that create the ball of clay, and then helps mold the clay into a compelling shape. The unsung hero.

And to the KBB Team, another group of unsung heroes who do the impossible while making it look like just another day: Juan Flores, Annette Rodriguez, Tina Saghafi, Rhonda Matini, Susie Beard (honorary KBB ☺), Grant Kemen, Carmen Long, Kevin Pham, Matt "Captain Picard" Bateman, Jennifer Wang, Caren Corliss, Matt Whiteside, Craig Combel, Alec Gutierrez, Michael Amore, Courtney Wilcock, Norman Lawson, Brian Vaziri, John Woo-Sam, John Beck, Justin Deshaw and Brenna Buehler.

With great support from Nichole Mrasek, Jeri Reichel, Mike Wulf, Dave Templeton, Jai Macker, Colin MacGillivray, Scott Freeland, Nathan Fox, Sean Stott, Lisa Aloisio, Karuna Koy, Mr. Mark Schirmer, along with great partnering from Team Xtime and the incredible vision and sponsorship of Paul Whitworth.

# Table of Contents

# Introduction

I've been working with dealers for almost 35 years in fixed operations. I've had the great fortune of starting or being involved in several technology companies that were very successful in helping fixed ops.

And while I've never drawn a paycheck from a dealer, I've worked with well more than 2,000 of them, observing the best operations around the country and taking part in implementing many new processes and technologies that produced great results -- and a few that didn't. I count many dealers and dealer personnel as friends.

I previously gave my view about the future needs of automotive service in a book I wrote last year, *Fast Lane: How to Accelerate Service Loyalty and Unlock Its Profit-Making Potential.* So why write another book?

A couple of reasons. First, our industry is changing at a faster pace than I've ever seen in my 35 years as a participant and close observer, and most of you tell me you see the same thing.

Second and most important, I've come to believe that many dealers have a blind spot about their service departments that must be corrected — urgently. We're transaction-centric, overly focused on the RO and on optimizing the dollars from each customer visit.

I understand why this happened: It's an outgrowth of the showroom, where we try to optimize the vehicle-sale transaction. But I believe this approach in service has caused, and continues to cause, great harm to overall dealer health.

What we need to focus on is how to keep every customer possible, so we can realize the most from their lifetime spend in service and sales.

In basketball, a fast break occurs when the ball quickly changes possession, and players move fast for a scoring opportunity. You quickly change from defense to offense. A fast break can sometimes be a game-changer.

The fast break is a fitting analogy for what I think will be an ever-more pressing need for dealers and service leaders to quickly break from the transaction-centric tradition and adopt a more customer-centric operating philosophy.

Unlike basketball, the fast break in your service operation won't happen in a matter of seconds. But I believe the commitment to make this important transition needs to come sooner rather than later, given the imminent changes to the car business — and the way we service cars and customers — that the future will most certainly bring.

If you imagine creating a customer-centric organization as drawing a bulls-eye with the customer in the center, we're currently not even aiming at that target. We're about 10 feet to the left, shooting at a different target that says "transaction-centric."

We must shift our aim so that we achieve the first-layer fundamentals (Culture, People, Leadership, Capacity, Facilities and Technology), then the elements they support, so that we're laser-focused on the customer.

My goal is that *Fast Break* gives you the framework and motivation to make the change and some tools to help you do it.

Ready? Then let's get to work.

# Chapter 1

## Are We Really Meeting Our Profitable Growth Objective?

For years I've been asking dealers and service leaders a question: "What's your primary objective in your service department?"

I'll often hear answers that are similar: "Happy customers" or "Customers who come back" or "top CSI scores."

I don't hear too many dealers or service leaders list "profitable growth" as a primary objective.

You could argue, I suppose, that the common answers imply profitable growth—that is, if you keep your customers happy and satisfied, they will come back.

But I take a different view.

I don't think that our industry, by and large, is optimizing the service-customer experience to the degree it could or should, and the consequences of this reality are only becoming more profound.

Let's start with some stats:

If you look at fixed-operations stats from NADA, you see what might be a troubling trend.

Since 2010, we've seen fixed operations log largely consistent annual growth rates of 4 percent to 6 percent. (In this stretch, there's a 1.1-percent decline between 2011 and 2012; it seems an anomaly amid the larger trend.)

If you look deeper, you'll see the industry achieved significant 8-percent growth in fixed operations in 2016—the largest lift in the past nearly 10-year stretch. If we think back to all of the airbag-related recalls that year, I think we can explain why dealership service departments logged more work.

But since that year, fixed-operations growth has been more modest.

In 2017, NADA says fixed operations across franchised dealerships grew about 3 percent. As 2018 comes to a close, it's looking like it'll be another year of 3-percent growth.

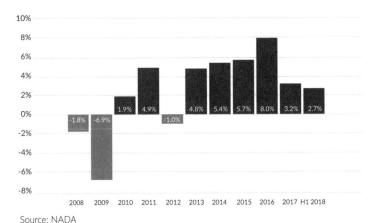

## Fixed Operations Continues to Grow
### Fixed Operations Growth

| Year | Value |
|------|-------|
| 2008 | -1.8% |
| 2009 | -6.9% |
| 2010 | 1.9% |
| 2011 | 4.9% |
| 2012 | -1.0% |
| 2013 | 4.8% |
| 2014 | 5.4% |
| 2015 | 5.7% |
| 2016 | 8.0% |
| 2017 | 3.2% |
| H1 2018 | 2.7% |

Source: NADA

I'm not suggesting this growth is bad. Far from it. Any growth, in any business, is a step in the right direction.

I would suggest, however, that there's a little more to the "growth" story we should be thinking about.

Let's take a step back for a moment, and consider a couple more questions:

Isn't it a little curious that fixed-operations growth in the past few years tracks very closely to the respective annual rates of growth in new vehicle sales?

Is it unfair, courageous or crazy to suggest that, with all the new vehicles and customers dealers have put on the roads for nearly the past decade, we should see even better growth rates?

Going a step further, isn't it reasonable to think that if one of our primary concerns is customer retention—as evidenced by nearly 57 percent of dealerships saying it is, in fact, a primary concern—then maybe, just maybe, we're not doing the job of retaining customers as well as we could or should?

Now, let's ask a different but related question: Has this recent growth really been profitable?

On one hand, the answer is absolutely.

If you look at NADA stats, you'll see that fixed operations is contributing a larger share of dealership gross profits for most stores—up from 45 percent in 2012 to 49 percent in 2017. (NADA's projections suggest the fixed-operations contribution to dealership gross profits ran about 49 percent in 2018, too.)

Meanwhile, through this same period, service revenues have remained stable at roughly 12 percent of overall dealership revenues.

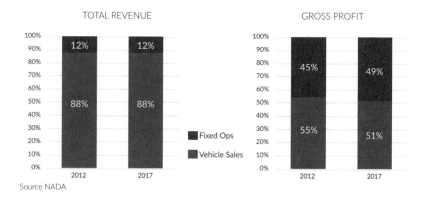

Source NADA

These numbers seem pretty good and healthy until you start considering that gross profits have been continuing to decline in new- and used-vehicle departments in recent years, even as revenues grow.

Against this backdrop, wouldn't it be reasonable to expect that if we really were achieving profitable growth in fixed operations, we'd see a more profound lift in both fixed-operations revenues and its contribution to total dealership gross profits?

All of this suggests to me that something is most definitely wrong.

We don't really seem to be retaining as many customers as we rightfully should, given our track record of new- and used-vehicle sales. And, since we aren't retaining customers as optimally as we might, we aren't really achieving the goal of truly profitable growth, year after year.

I feel the need to call this situation exactly what it is—a sign of significant *underperformance* in fixed operations, no matter what the official statistics appear to suggest.

It's my belief that the primary reason behind this underperformance is the way we service (or don't service) our service customers.

By and large, it seems our customers exist to serve our purposes of selling more hours and work to make more money (the transaction-centric mindset) rather than truly serving customers to develop the trust and loyalty that will keep them coming back and not leaving us for good (the customer-centric mindset).

## *The goal is profitable growth.*

In the following chapters, we'll examine how you can make a fast break toward a more customer-centric operating philosophy and, perhaps more important, why this philosophy is essential to adopt today, before the chance for you to make your break passes you by.

For now, though, I'd respectfully suggest that we stop kidding ourselves. Yes, as an industry, we might be growing in fixed operations and, yes, we might be making money.

But I think you'll agree that we could and should do better. The opportunity to achieve profitable growth, year after year, is out there.

My question to you is whether you'll have the fortitude and will to seize this opportunity for you and your customers.

# Chapter 2

## A Tougher Road Ahead

**F**ast breaks in basketball don't happen if players are standing on their heels.

That's why coaches, in basketball or any other sport where reaction time and speed are critical factors, implore young players to stay on their toes. To be up and ready to move. All the time.

I share this analogy because it's fitting for the situation where today's dealers and service leaders find themselves. I believe we are in the car business's equivalent of a fast-break moment when it comes to adopting a customer-centric operating philosophy in fixed operations.

We have a choice. We have the option to either react to the moment, or it will pass.

Now, I consider myself a pretty even-keeled, level-headed person.

In fact, I got my pilot's license in part because flying a plane requires an ultimate degree of control. Even in dire, panic-prone situations, it's the steady hand and mind that keeps the plane in the sky or gets it, and your passengers, safely back to ground.

In other words, I wouldn't suggest that we are in a somewhat urgent moment for fixed operations if I didn't truly believe the time to transition to a customer-centric operating philosophy is upon us.

This urgency is rooted in the current and emerging realities of the auto-retailing environment:

### Reality: Dealers will expect better results than you're delivering to ensure the overall health of their dealership investments.

It's no secret that margin compression on the variable side of your dealership is significant these days. The average gross margin for new-vehicle sales declined to 2.5 percent in 2017, from 3.3 percent in 2015 and a whopping 4.6 percent as recently as 2011, according to NADA data. On a net basis, most dealers now are losing money selling new vehicles.

Meanwhile, used-vehicle gross profits as a percentage of transaction prices continue to slide, down to an average 11.7 percent in 2017 from 13.7 percent in 2011, according to NADA.

And for the first time in the memories of anyone I know, the average retail net profit in used vehicles went negative in 2017, sliding to a -$2. Of course, one of the primary drivers for this result is that luxury brands miscalculated residual values of vehicles coming off lease, which forced dealers to buy them back for more than they could be sold at retail.

Join those grim statistics to the fact that we've probably peaked on the sales side. Indeed, it looks like the industry is experiencing a soft landing, but we're still going to be selling fewer vehicles and making less money as we do.

I suspect many dealers are viewing these financial stats with the same reaction as Scooby-Doo on a Saturday morning: "Ruh-roh."

The bottom line is that dealers will, out of necessity, be leaning more heavily than ever on fixed operations to drive the financial results they expect from their stores.

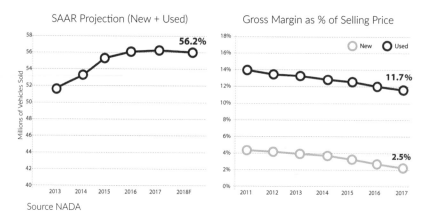

Source NADA

**Reality: A different set of customer expectations**: The financial pressures on dealerships are occurring at the same time as the fundamental relationship between American consumers and the process of buying an automobile continues to shift.

For good reason, Americans have come to regard the car-buying experience on a par with getting teeth pulled on the list of unpleasant episodes in their lives — thanks to the time it takes to complete the purchase, the annoying persistence of price haggling, and other aspects of the transaction that spell aggravation, apprehension and tension for buyers.

So, if there were "reverse bucket lists" of experiences that most Americans would want to avoid until the day they die, surely "dealing with the new-car-buying process" would be at or near the top of many lists.

The general distaste for the car-buying experience hasn't been lost on a growing body of entrepreneurs. There are plenty of companies offering alternatives to the traditional car-buying experience. (Car vending machines are a neat gimmick.)

Meanwhile, dealers are playing catch-up. After years of pooh-poohing or scoffing at the idea, dealers are now recognizing that a digitally driven sales process isn't just something for the future, its time has arrived today.

Consumers can access any number of vehicle-research sites and can browse inventory online. The dealer, OEM and third parties are integrating their processes—for example, the credit application is online and helps speed lending decisions; other portions of the F&I process have been moved online or streamlined to reduce customer wait times; test drives can be scheduled online; and you can even make deposits prior to stepping foot in the dealership.

These advances in digital retailing lessen the Number One pain point of the vehicle purchase: time spent in the dealership. By blending traditional processes with online options, consumers can now tailor the purchasing process to their satisfaction.

This digital evolution in sales signals a must-change moment for fixed operations. If the sales side of the dealership is embracing technology to better meet customer expectations, shouldn't the same be true in service? Or, conversely, if your sales department still offers a 1980s or 1990s-era sales process, is it reasonable to expect that you'll even see these customers in your service lanes?

**Reality: Vehicles last longer and run better.** On one hand, you might look at the time today's consumers typically own their vehicles and see a wealth of opportunity. Dealers and their service departments, theoretically, ought to have more opportunities to engage and serve customers who are driving the vehicles they purchased from the dealership.

But it's not that simple.

## Vehicles Are Expected to Last Longer than Ever Before
### Length of Ownership & Vehicle Age Continue to Climb

| AVERAGE LENGTH OF OWNERSHIP | AVERAGE AGE OF VEHICLES ON THE ROAD |
|---|---|
| 2008 · 2018 | 2008 · 2018 |
| 46 → 79 | 10 → 12 |
| MONTHS · MONTHS | YEARS · YEARS |

Source: IHS/Markit

For starters, according to J.D. Power & Associates, vehicle quality has been steadily increasing for decades now: Cars break less often, so there are fewer needs for repairs. This is true across the industry, and today the few brands that are still considered marginal players nevertheless demonstrate very good fit, finish and reliability.

Also, while manufacturing quality has been steadily improving, OEMs have been able to design vehicles that need routine service far less often. Maintenance intervals have been steadily increasing over the last 15 years, so the good old, "3 months/3,000 miles" rule is long gone.

Other factors keep our customers out of our service bays. For example, with some brands there is significant leasing, and those vehicles are serviced a little less often because owners don't have the long-term health of the vehicle in mind.

It also looks like recall activity is expected to drop slightly compared with the last couple of years, when recall visits to dealerships spiked due to some major campaigns. Consider that the ignition-switch and Takata air-bag issues alone affected millions of vehicles.

Also, we'll be seeing more over-the-air updates of software, of the kind that Tesla has pioneered—one less reason for a vehicle owner to come back to you.

It's also true that electric vehicles will gain more share and you don't have to look much beyond a Tesla owner's manual to understand what it means for factory-recommended maintenance intervals. The manual recommends maintenance for a Tesla. There aren't many pages in that manual.

You probably already know why electric vehicles need fewer technician touch points. These vehicles have an estimated 70 percent fewer moving parts than their gasoline-powered counterparts.

Add it up, and nowadays, I think we can figure on seeing a vehicle owner in our service departments only once every 10,000 to 12,000 miles, which on average is about once per year.

**Reality: Stiffer competition**. Already, dealers have faced stiffer competition from aftermarket service providers including Pep Boys, Midas and the like.

I think it's fair to say that our traditional, transaction-centric operating philosophy has helped the loss of business to what some of you consider aftermarket interlopers. Part of the story also owes to the rise of online options that help vehicle owners easily research and find non-dealership service providers.

Whatever the cause, I think we can all agree the aftermarket providers have hurt dealers badly in two ways.

First, over the decades, they have done an incredibly good job of convincing consumers that OEM dealers are unnecessarily expensive. Even though most research shows that dealers have become very cost-competitive, that's not the story these chains tell the vehicle-owning public. And, of course, many American consumers have bought the story.

The other thing these chains have done, more recently, is very smart as well: They've shed the specialization that used to define their marketplaces and mostly have become generalists that compete more effectively with car dealers for service work. For example, 44 percent of independent-service-center profits come from tire mounting and balancing, brake service, chassis and suspension work, and not from their core products and services, according to *Modern Tire Dealer* magazine.

Play a quick name-association game and you'll understand what I mean. I'll name a brand, and immediately a specific type of service will come to your mind—the same one that always used to come to consumers' minds. Midas and Meineke? Mufflers. Firestone and Goodyear? Of course, tires.

But now, these chains and others have evolved into providing general automotive maintenance, not just their traditional specialties. Like the quick-lube chains, they're going after the preventative-maintenance trade that used to go mainly to car dealers' service departments.

There is some encouraging news for dealerships on this front. In 2017, dealerships raised their share of consumer service visits to 33 percent of the industry, up from 30 percent the year before.[1]

That's a significant increase.

And from whom did dealers take that share? Mostly from the quick-lube places that comprised a significant new wave of competition when they began proliferating 20 years ago or so.

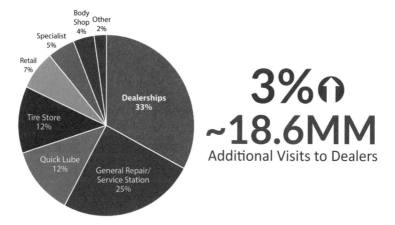

Last year, quick-lube businesses lost share, down to 12 percent from 14 percent in 2016.[2]

It's likely that a rise in warranties and recalls, coupled with good selling practices by dealers, were largely responsible for the decline at quick-lube places. Three of five visits to the dealership in 2017 included an oil change, Cox Automotive research shows. Many of them included an additional service such as tire rotations.

[1] Source: Cox Automotive 2018 Service Industry Study.
[2] Source: Ibid

I view all of this as positive progress. But I wonder if the market share-retaking momentum is moving fast enough, particularly when you consider the non-brick-and-mortar players who are now part of our competitive landscape. Let's consider Amazon's entry into the business of selling aftermarket parts and, in some cases, the services to install those parts.

Two years ago, Amazon launched its Amazon Vehicles page, setting off great speculation that the e-commerce titan was going after new-vehicle sales. I think it's more likely Amazon is pursuing automotive advertising.

But there's no doubt what Amazon has been doing in the service business: It entered the replacement parts and accessories space in 2017, competing with parts stores such as Advance and O'Reilly as well as with dealers. Amazon is experimenting with selling tires and other components online and arranging for installation at chain service centers as well.

Amazon also has rolled out something called Amazon Home Services in select areas of the country, where customers can order new tires, brake-pad or -shoe replacement, wheel alignment, rim installation and even vehicle-backup cameras installed at your home or business by contractors Amazon has lined up.

## Writing on the Wall

I hope that this run-through of risks to our collective status quo helps underscore the urgency I mentioned earlier to shift to a more customer-centric operating philosophy.

Some of you might make the case that none of these factors pose an imminent risk to your business. Yes, each one is bubbling along, but your current course rests on fairly solid ground.

This is true, of course. But I would offer two considerations that might help you rethink your sense of urgency:

First, the bubbles could boil at any moment. Let's say that retail vehicle sales fall more precipitously than the experts expect. What will that mean for your ability to drive profitable growth?

Second, it's easier to make significant strategic shifts in your business—like fast-breaking toward a customer-centric operating philosophy—when business is relatively good. When you're in crisis mode, it's nearly impossible to be as thoughtful, disciplined and patient about making any big change to your business. In most cases, times of crisis push us all to our comfort zones, which is rarely an incubator for innovation.

*The time to repair the roof is when the sun is shining.*

Before we dig into the specifics of how you can execute your own shift to a customer-centric operating philosophy, we need to address another very real risk to your ability to succeed in tomorrow's service business.

This risk is different than all the ones I've outlined in this chapter. It's not an external risk; it's internal. It goes to very heart of how you regard your customers and what they mean for the future of your business.

# Chapter 3

## Your Own Worst Enemy

You don't have to convince Steve Nicholson, director of operations at Temecula (CA) Hyundai that a customer-centric operating philosophy is a better way—for him, it's the only way.

"I have one simple, guiding concept," says Nicholson, taking a cue from one of Vince Lombardi's famous credos. "Customer service isn't everything—it's the only thing. I've lived my life by it; honestly, that's it."

Nicholson considers his perspective a competitive advantage.

"So many people in our industry will find a reason to look at the customer and say, 'My job isn't to see it your way but to get you to see it my way.' But we need to look at everything through the eyes of that customer."

---

*"So many people in our industry will find a reason to look at the customer and say, 'My job isn't to see it your way but to get you to see it my way.' But we need to look at everything through the eyes of that customer."*

---

"Other dealers want to try to make as much money as they can from every customer," Nicholson says. "But in parts and service we have the opposite philosophy of that. If you pound someone on an RO like they get pounded in the sales department, you'll never see that customer again. Rather than take a lot from a few, we want to gain a little from a lot. We want to see the customer more than once."

I've shared Nicholson's perspective because it's a spot-on assessment of the prevalence of the transaction-centric mindset that defines the way many dealers and service leaders run their parts and service businesses.

It's all about the money, not about the way you might make your money.

This sounds pretty easy on paper. But I think we can all agree that undoing a hard-wired tradition of viewing customers as dollar signs isn't easy.

Darrel Ferguson sees this dollar-sign problem first hand.

He started in the business in 1989 and worked as a GM and minority partner in a Texas-based Toyota store which was part of a dealer group. He now heads up a group of performance managers working with dealers to help them break toward a more customer-centric operating philosophy.

"Dealers have to divorce their traditions, all these bad habits they've developed over 80 years or so," Ferguson says. "We've operated with the opposite of transparency and are now coming into the modern world kicking and screaming."

The most troubling part of the transaction-centric operating philosophy is that today's customers can see it, or at least sense it a mile away.

If you review service satisfaction surveys, most customers today can't articulate exactly why they feel dissatisfied—but that's beside the point. They *are* dissatisfied. They aren't sure if they paid a fair and reasonable price, or their valuable time wasn't treated respectfully. Or they felt the experience was out of step with the times. These are the seeds that lead to defection.

The transaction-centric approach certainly may pad the profitability of a particular customer visit—but it risks losing that customer for life.

For dealers and service leaders, adding a few hundred dollars to an RO that isn't really necessary doesn't seem like such a big deal. But, for today's customers, it's often a lifelong deal breaker.

"We practice the same old pattern in service. We draw in the customer with an offer of a $29 oil change, and an hour after they arrive the service advisor is taking a knee next to them in the waiting room," Ferguson says. "He's trying to upsell a $500 RO. We really have been, and often remain, our own executioners."

By now, many of you may be wondering exactly why a transaction-centric operating philosophy is out of step with today's vehicle buyers and owners.

In fact, I suspect many of you already know the answers, but let's drill down a bit to make sure we're all on the same page.

The reality is that today's customer expectations are being shaped by the experiences they get in other retail environments. As these new expectations develop, it's only natural that today's vehicle buyers and owners bring them to your dealership's showroom or service door.

Consumers—especially the millennial generation who are today's fastest growing cohort of car buyers—have gotten used to a new type of commercial transaction and brand relationships in all other areas of their lives.

Most of the changes, of course, have come because of the vastly transformative effects of digital technology. It enables brands to create convenient, often inexpensive, customized, contextualized and networked interactions with consumers that please and delight them in the moment and have the secondary effect—though primary purpose—of engendering their loyalty in a long-term relationship with a brand.

And because of these experiences happening outside of automotive, consumers' expectations of the auto business, specifically, have risen dramatically too.

All of Americans' new experiences with digital platforms in other areas of their lives have made them expect the same kind of revolution in the auto industry.

You don't have to look too far to see how destructive this changing set of customer expectations can be for traditional retail businesses—think Sears, Toys R' Us, Bon Ton, and many more. They're all gone because they failed to provide the retail experience today's customers demand.

Think about it: Any parent can sit in their apartment, condo or home and order a gross of diapers, a pair of left-handed scissors, a $200 silk tie, a bag of organic cat food, and a leather couch and have them all appear on their doorstep, sometimes the same day.

The reason Amazon has taken over so much of retailing isn't just that it has unmatched selection of merchandise at unmatched prices but also that it has put so much effort into painstaking details that make the purchase process frictionless.

At every turn, Amazon's purpose is to make transactions simpler and more intuitive. Customers respond with loyalty that is the envy of every retailer, and Amazon has been able to turn the business world upside down. And now they're a trillion-dollar company.

Millennials, and the rest of us, also can pick a restaurant online via Open Table, and get a no-hassle dinner reservation for this evening without having to talk to someone through a bad phone connection, with loud background music and distracting background conversations.

Getting a reservation used to be one of the most annoying aspects of a typical customer's relationship with any restaurant. You had to call the place, and if you really wanted a specific time and date, you had to call far ahead. Often your preferred slot wasn't available, and so you had to jockey with the restaurant host over the phone for another time, imagining an Excel spreadsheet in your head.

But with the introduction of Open Table, now you can schedule a restaurant reservation yourself, online, with a few clicks. You can see the same availability information that the host does. And the restaurant has removed one of the greatest sources of friction with its customers. Now they just make sure that, when you show up, they seat you when they've promised.

A great example from the transportation industry is Delta Airlines: Fliers can use its app to complete a very complex reservation experience, then to get through airport security, then to board the plane—and now the app even will tell you when your baggage has been loaded onto and then off the jet.

In a business where, traditionally, customers have been so easily frustrated, such convenience and transparency has helped Delta to be rated consistently as one of the best domestic flying experiences, and that has secured loyalty with travelers.

Now heading even closer to home, an incredibly transformative consumer experience was created in the last decade by Uber and Lyft.

Not only did these digital ride-sharing services vastly improve the old alternative-transportation business built around taxis, but the ease of the customer experience, and the relationships that riders are building with these brands, has completely altered the course of a decades-old industry that reigned for more than a century.

One of my favorite aspects of this phenomenon: Uber didn't even invent any new technologies. They combined mobile, GPS and social media and presto—a new and improved customer experience.

Uber has managed to parlay a vastly improved customer relationship into a staggering corporate valuation of as much as $120 billion for an initial public offering that Uber planned for early 2019, the *Wall Street Journal* estimated.

There's another consideration: The increasingly technological nature of many everyday items, including the car, is leading consumers to believe that the auto industry should be delivering a technology-enhanced experience utilizing the sort of technical wizardry it is displaying in the vehicle.

After all, if the industry can design a machine that is capable of automatically warning you about an imminent collision or fender bender; if carmakers can design engines that stop and start almost seamlessly in the interest of boosting fuel economy and cutting emissions while idling—why can't consumers expect the same levels of technological sophistication and user-friendliness when it comes to the dealership service experience?

Indeed, all these other developments in our industry nudge customers in the direction of wanting more technology involved in the relationship between them and the people who service and repair these highly sophisticated machines.

This reality has spurred some dealers and service leaders to work even harder to keep up with changing customer expectations.

"Periodically, we hold innovation meetings to look for opportunities to keep up with current technology," says Jack Turske, the Fixed Operations Director of Fox Motors. "Due to the faced-paced environment our dealership employees work in, it is not hard to see why they are more comfortable using what they know instead of looking for new and more customer-centric ways of servicing their customers. As leaders, it is our responsibility to stay on top of the technology curve."

Everything I've just described is shaping and changing the way that today's customers expect to be treated in every brand and commercial relationship now and in the future.

And, if we're all honest, these things are changing our own expectations for retail experiences. If you're anything like me, you've come to believe that if I'm online or in a store, the focus had better be on me, or else.

I don't think it's unreasonable to suggest that if we expect this kind of experience for ourselves, shouldn't we extend it to our customers? And, if we don't, and choose to maintain a transaction-centric operating philosophy, can we really expect to be relevant and viable fixed-operations providers in the future?

It should also be pointed out that if we choose not to make the shift to a customer-centric operating philosophy, the risks are higher, because it's become much easier for unhappy customers to shape public opinion about the way we do business.

It doesn't take long in this era of Yelp and other viral social media for just a few negative reviews of a dealership to create a really bad reputation, especially if the complaints come from not customers who merely didn't like the coffee in the waiting room, or who tell the world about your rude service writer—but those who felt that they got shafted and complain about the experience.

In this environment, it seems to me that while breaking with tradition, and moving to a more customer-centric operating philosophy may mean disruption and some risk, the alternative poses a much greater threat to your business. The fact is, if you want to be relevant for tomorrow's customers, who will have less direct need to come to your dealership, it's a good idea to start giving today's customers more reasons to stay with you rather than leave.

OK. Enough of the convincing. If you don't yet see the value of creating a customer-centric operating philosophy, you might ask taxi company owners for their thoughts.

For the rest of us, let's, let's get into the nuts and bolts of making the break, and building a customer-centric operating philosophy.

### Key Takeaways:

- Some dealers are changing, but many have stuck with a transaction orientation instead of becoming customer-centric.
- Technology-enhanced experiences are driving higher customer expectations.
- The auto business needs to keep pace with those expectations by transforming the traditional experience in its dealerships.

# Chapter 4

## Your Fast Break Framework

It's fun to watch a well-executed fast break in basketball.

I'm not talking about the fast breaks where a player strips the ball and has a clean run to the basket, and hopefully a strong, maybe even flashy, finish.

I'm talking about the multi-player fast breaks. Where something—like a stripped or tipped ball—triggers a chain reaction. Players pivot and change direction. The offensive players fan out to create a multi-point attack and spread the defensive players.

Ideally, the offensive players pass the ball to the person with the best shot, who scores.

The well-executed fast break is a good analogy for what it takes to make your own break from a transaction-centric operating philosophy to one that's customer-centric.

But before you can begin to build your own model to execute a customer-centric operating philosophy, you've got to agree that it's necessary. And true customer appreciation doesn't necessarily come naturally to this industry.

I was speaking to a group of service managers in Chicago recently about what customers expect from service departments, and one of the guys stood up. He was talking about something that didn't occur, say, in the 1980s, but what he did a few months ago.

This service manager met with all of his service advisors, and he taught all of them how to … shake hands. Then, when they had that down pat—and it actually took a couple of weeks—he taught them how to look people in the eye and smile.

This is a great example of re-evaluating the basics through the customers' eyes. And I'm sure this story resonates with a lot of service managers.

The lesson here is we're still an industry ripe for understanding how to put the customer at the center, and this involves the fundamentals of human relationships, some of the basic things that have been true since the beginning—not just figuring out how to use the latest digital technologies.

In fact, embracing the customer will require a bigger investment than just getting employees to watch a YouTube video on how to shake hands—although that may be a great starting point.

In order to truly put the customer at the center of your operation and your future, dealers must evolve their business model. You must put customer loyalty on a pedestal above everything else, and above any other objectives. You must make customer retention the bulls-eye and keep shooting at it until the arrow lands there every time.

Ramzy Handal, vice president of fixed operations for Jim Koons Automotive, which has 16 rooftops in Maryland, Virginia, Delaware and Washington, D.C., is among the growing number of enlightened service managers and dealers who agree with me.

"Where we fail as dealers is our retention numbers," he says. "I'd rather spend $3,000 to retain my own customers that I sold versus spend $2,000 to find new customers in my PMA. If my retention number across stores is 90 percent, then, yeah—I'll spend some money on new business.

"So that's my reasoning: Why would I go out and spend money to bring in new business? Let's just worry about, 'How can I retain what I sold in my showroom?'"

I've always wondered why more dealers don't already take a customer-centric approach like this. Most of our revenue flows from the customers, so why haven't we treated them like the tangible assets they are?

You spend a lot of time evaluating the financial statements and related metrics of your business. You should consider your customer base as much of an asset as you do your new-vehicle, used-vehicle and parts inventories.

In fact, if dealers spent as much time optimizing customers in the same way they do other assets, you'd probably provide a much better experience. Because when you have an asset, you track, analyze and optimize. Most OEM's have UOI analyses available for service customers–but when was the last time you looked at those? Not only the current report, but the historical reports for comparison. How is your customer base doing? Is it growing or shrinking?

If a dealer's objective is lifetime wallet share, looking at customers as an asset would seem to merit serious consideration.

We need to recast our thinking toward lifetime value, with a service-customer-centric view.

## A Virtuous Customer-Centric Circle

I've constructed a simple model you should have in mind as you begin the work of building your own customer-centric operating philosophy. It's a picture to shape your view of the elements and structure, and the way they work together, to create a truly customer-centric dealership.

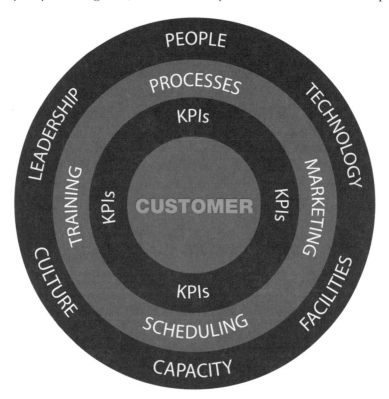

The model offers a series of concentric circles that represent a customer-centric dealership. You must work your way from the outside of the circle towards the center. In the defining Outer Circle are the foundational elements, the crucial components that must encircle everything else for the model to work.

Those elements are Leadership, Culture, People, Capacity, Facilities, and Technology—these are the fundamental building blocks, the table stakes, if you will, for creating customer-centricity.

Inside that circle rests a second circle, consisting of the elements that are closer to the customer, that express and support the fundamental components in the Outer Circle.

In that Inner Circle are Processes, Training, Scheduling and Marketing. Each is a complement of the elements in the Outer Circle in helping create a customer-centric dealership.

And moving closer to the center, in a third circle, are KPIs—Key Performance Indicators—that tell you how your dealership is doing in creating a customer-centric environment. In some cases, these KPIs are different than those you have probably used in the past.

Of course, in the very center of these concentric circles, of course—both literally and figuratively—is the customer. The customer is the center of your customer-centric dealership.

And if you place customers there, they will reward you with lifetime relationships that will result in more sales and service business and continued prosperity.

If the customer isn't at the very middle, if something else occupies the focus of your dealership, then you're focusing on the wrong things.

With this model in mind, first let's look at the elements of the Outer Circle that you must line up around the entire enterprise and at some ways in which the pieces of the Inner Circle complement and express those fundamentals around the customer. Then we'll take a look at the components of that Inner Circle.

## Leadership

The first essential element of the encompassing circle is Leadership. The leaders in building customer-centric dealerships, the enlightened fixed-ops directors, service managers, general managers and dealership principals.

A break to a customer-centric dealership may start any of a number of ways, with one new practice, or one enlightened manager.

But while such factors may move the needle a bit on the dealership's success with customer retention, the only way to get a full-on transformation is when it is committed to by the leaders of your organization.

Consider how some of the pioneers of customer-centric service departments, leaders who've put their livelihoods and reputations— and their dealerships, in some cases—on the line describe their approach.

The leader of the large midwestern dealer group, says the group's emphasis on customers starts with its CEO.

"From day one, he's expected everybody who ever touches the customer to be customer-centric," says the leader of the large midwestern dealer group. "He's wanted us to focus on making the experience the best that it can be for customers, and how to use innovation to do that."

Leaders at Del Grande Dealer Group find ways to explain their conviction to their employees.

"For us it's not about hours per RO, it's about treating guests like you'd treat your mother," says Tully Williams, former head of service for the dealership operation in California. "Why would I sell something to you that I wouldn't sell to my mother?"

Another trailblazer in creating customer-centric experiences agrees.

"It's crucial because customers dictate your long-term success," says Trevor Gile, general manager of the Motorcars Group, which owns Toyota and Honda dealerships in metro Cleveland.

"You have to create experiences that continue to wow them, that meet or exceed their expectations. Otherwise they're going to go somewhere else, and the competition will gain ground."

Look at Hilton Head Honda, a small dealership on the tony resort island of Hilton Head, South Carolina. Service manager Marno Muth has been at work on the biggest fast break this dealership had ever made.

And after investing hundreds of thousands of dollars in facilities expansion and overhaul, and in new technology to run service appointments, Hilton Head Honda sees the way clear to a vibrant future despite all the headwinds.

That's because they've put their customers at the center of their operation, so they can drive big growth.

"My biggest challenge was taking a small dealership that wanted big-dealership numbers and convincing them, hey, you have to spend some money [in fixed operations] to be able to keep up with these guys," Muth tells me. "Keep up with the bigger dealers in the metro areas and keep up with the demand that they're able to take in."

## Culture

This element falls largely to dealers and their service leaders. Once you've made the choice to break to a customer-centric operating philosophy, it'll be on you to determine what the supporting Culture will look like, and the type of people you'll need to execute your new approach to and vision for your customers.

The definition of business culture is generally accepted to be "the beliefs and behaviors that determine how a company's employees and leadership interact and handle business transactions."

Once you've decided to be on the customer-centric path, if you don't already have a culture built around the customer it will take some time to evolve your organization in that direction.

Have you heard the story about the company president who gathered the management team together and said, "I've been thinking a lot about company culture—have one in place by next week, OK"?

If only it were so easy! But as management guru and former General Electric CEO Jack Welch once famously put it, "The soft stuff is the hard stuff."

Hiring the right people is crucial to make a cultural overhaul work. Of course, training these same people is essential as well, not just in diagnostics and repair improvements for the techs but also for teaching customer-centric ways and underscoring their importance.

Effective training is one of the best ways to build on the solid fundamentals of a customer-centric culture and a customer-centric workforce.

And it's a way to ensure that day-in, day-out practices at your dealership are all, and always, putting the customer at the center.

## People

The third major element of our Outer Circle is People—and by that, I mean hiring and keeping the right people. In this day and age of rising consumer expectations, you need to make sure your team is full of individuals who will put the customer at the center of everything they do.

Generally, becoming customer-centric requires service departments to be as concerned about interacting with consumers as they are with achieving excellence in the technical aspects of their operation.

The Number One quality service leaders look for in today's service advisor is empathy—that ability to understand and share the feelings of others. And this means hiring and promoting service advisors who have great communication skills and empathy—who are modeled on the neighborhood coffee barista, for example.

New-era employees also need to be open-minded, adaptable and flexible, because the automotive environment is changing quickly. People not comfortable with change are often uncomfortable in these environments, and they can degrade the customer experience.

Additionally, they must be comfortable with today's cloud-based mobile technology, and fortunately, most millennials are.

For these reasons, the days of a highly competent technician simply transferring over to become a service advisor are less likely; their core competencies and the most important needs of a customer-centric advisor probably won't match up with your optimal technician profile.

You may need to modernize your hiring practices to ensure you're bringing in the right type of people. Pay close attention to previous work experience—did they work with customers? Use personality profiling as part of your hiring practices—ensure to test for the qualities that a customer-centric hire must have.

And make sure you put your hiring prospects through multiple interviews with different people in the dealership. Seeing how your candidates fare with various personality types is an important checkpoint in getting the right type of people.

## Capacity

A lack of Capacity is the enemy of retention. No customer wants to be told that they have to wait one to two weeks to get their vehicle serviced, especially if it's an urgent situation. Like an air-conditioning problem in July in Florida or when a customer needs a vehicle to start a family vacation on schedule.

The general agreement of service leaders is that two days should be your target for taking care of repair-related items and for routine maintenance, while you should be able to accommodate emergency requests immediately.

Correction of recalled vehicles is included in the two- day bucket as well, in part because the news media's reporting of recalls has raised consumer sensitivity to safety concerns.

And if a dealership doesn't have a slot available, customers will either find someone else who does or hold a grudge. When a customer wants to get something done, they can't be told to come back in two weeks when a dealership has an opening.

Even if it's a matter of routine maintenance and nothing close to an emergency, they may take their business elsewhere—if only because getting that car-repair appointment is at the top of their to-do list today, and they want to be able to check it off and move on to the next item.

Once in the dealership, if we can get you in and out in less than two and a half hours, research shows,[3] customers are OK with that. Consumers who are most satisfied with dealers—who say they are "very satisfied" and "I'll always go to them"—spend just 2.4 hours on average per visit.

If the average gets up to three hours, the typical customer says they're "somewhat satisfied" and "might use [the dealership] in the

[3] Source: Cox Automotive 2018 Service Industry Study

future." At 3.7 hours, customers say they're "very dissatisfied" and will "never go back" to that dealership.

## Consumers Who Are Most Satisfied Spend 2.5 Hours or Less at the Dealer for Service
### Consumer Time Spent (Hours)

| | |
|---|---|
| 👍 Very satisfied, I'll always go to them | **2.4** |
| Somewhat satisfied, I might use in the future | **3.0** |
| 👎 Very dissatisfied, I'll never go back | **3.7** |

Looking at capacity in a customer-centric way might prompt you to put a different set of considerations at the top of the pile when it comes to decisions about how to deploy and utilize capacity.

You probably aren't using all your existing capacity to its optimal potential to create customer-centric experiences.

Even if you're managing to optimize utilization with scheduling software, you may still need to add more capacity. You might consider paying employees overtime. Adding weekend hours. Outsourcing used-car reconditioning to free up on-site bays for service customers. Maybe adding a second shift. Or, finally, breaking ground on an expansion.

And if your inadequate capacity forces customers away, don't expect them to come back—ever. You're sacrificing the potential for lots of downstream revenue, and of course dealers know that it's always much easier to keep an existing customer than to obtain a new one.

You need to make room for that customer so they never become that ex-customer. And you need to take preventative actions in your most important business planning, shoring up that component of the outer circle.

## Facilities

Another foundational element of our outer circle and of a customer-centric experience is your Facilities. While I realize that re-tooling your facility extensively may be impractical, you can do lots of things to make it more customer-centric.

That's why a simple thing like exterior signage can actually be a very highly effective tool for pleasing customers. Not only do you need to have labeling and directions to where the service department is located, and how customers get there once they enter the dealership drive, but also: What should customers do when they get to the service drive? Park or pull in? Honk if the weather's bad? Do you have appointment versus non-appointment lanes? Quick lane or not?

Look through the customers' eyes, keeping in mind that they may never have been to your service department, and if they were previously, it may have been months or even years ago.

Here's a great experiment: Pull in with someone who's not in the automotive industry and has never been to your dealership (a nephew or niece, or a new acquaintance, maybe) and see how they do with navigating to the right spots.

Amenities are another important area for making facilities customer-centric, especially the service-waiting room. Not long ago, amenities might have consisted of a six-hours-old pot of coffee and one small TV on the wall.

But nowadays, in line with their higher expectations of other retail environments, service customers are looking for a high-quality experience while they wait, with Wi-Fi and clean, comfortable surroundings serving as mere table stakes.

Savvy dealers also will make waiting areas more appealing to female customers, because car-ownership rates continue to rise, and because many moms are service customers these days. It'll matter to them if you offer a children's play area and it's clean.

## Technology

Leveraging digital technology may not have been part of an outer circle at a customer-centric dealership even 10 years ago, but it certainly is now. Technology permeates every aspect of our lives. We've come to expect technology-enhanced experiences everywhere we go. Yet the automotive experience significantly lags other industries in using technology to drive a better experience and improve loyalty.

# 85.9% of dealers
## State that their current systems do not provide a superior ownership experience
Source: 2018 Xtime Market Research Study

"The vast majority of dealerships out there are probably average dealerships," says Robert Scott, corporate director of fixed operations for Bob Johnson Chevrolet in Rochester, New York. The good news is that new technology platforms "can work for average dealerships that are probably trying to get better."

With technology as a proxy for commitment to becoming a customer-centric dealership, adoption of new software platforms becomes indicative of where dealers and their management teams stand on this issue.

And success in execution reflects the overall excellence of the dealership. It's all about consistency and dedication.

"The excellent dealership can commit to unfolding technology over time," says Scott. "But I think the technology also works for the vast majority of us in the middle too. It just works better for those guys on the top side because they're great at implementing consistent processes all over the place.

"So, when you give them a tool that's pretty good and easy to track, you know, they're great at it ... But the consistency of action becomes challenging for some dealers who consider themselves pretty successful" and who may not be carefully considering their long-term prosperity.

"There are still a vast number of car dealers who don't spend any time on process. They just sort of roll open the doors and, you know, they're lucky to be a Honda dealership in Southern California. Their life has always been one of selling lots of cars, making lots of money. And so, they don't spend a whole lot of time thinking about how to put in new processes."

But even the best such technology isn't a panacea for a dealership that wants to become customer-centric. "You can't fix 'stupid' with technology, or a bad experience with technology," says Jim Coleman, a former dealer and service-operations executive for Ford. "It just becomes a worse experience with good technology."

Leveraging technology to enable a customer-centric dealership takes not only the best software but also a commitment from leadership through the ranks to make it work.

"Technology can be your best friend or your worst enemy," says Chris Ward, national director of fixed operations for Summit Automotive Partners, which has 12 rooftops in five states throughout the northeast, Tennessee and Colorado.

## *"Technology can be your best friend or your worst enemy."*

Turske, the Fixed Operations Director with responsibility for 25 dealerships in the Midwest, tells me, "Early on in the process, I had to really commit that we were going to make [a new technology platform] work. And the leadership team recognized that this was going to dramatically change how we monitor and metric our business, because previously we didn't have access to this type of reporting tool.

We've always been a metric and performance driven dealer group, but we've never had a tool that provides the data needed to fully analyze our fixed operations. We can see how effective each technician / advisor team is and know who is using the tools properly.

We are a group that uses metrics to analyze our operations in order to maximize dealership performance and provide a consistent experience for our customers."

Technology platforms must deliver a better, faster, and even delightful experience for your customer. And they must be so user-friendly that service writers, technicians and others in the dealership feel compelled—not forced—to use them. It's got to be a win-win-win solution for the customer, the dealership and the employee whom you expect to use it.

Take Todd Ruprecht, fixed-operations director at Koons of Silver Springs, a three-brand dealership in Silver Spring, MD. The dealership has partnered with a texting solution that enables nearly complete automation of sending and receiving text messages.

"Customers love it," Ruprecht says. "Most people text these days, and you don't need to interrupt what you're doing, you can read them when it's convenient. And it frees up the advisors from the phones, so they do a better job of taking care of the customers."

These days, systems in other industries work together seamlessly to deliver a holistic, integrated experience. The systems in automotive retail must deliver that same kind of unbroken experience.

At the same time, the technology must fit customer preferences. "Texting is the best way to communicate with most people now," says Williams, formerly of Del Grande Dealer Group. "We want to communicate what is wrong with the car in a way that isn't intrusive.

"That's what the customer wants, not what the dealer necessarily wants—they want to be communicated with their way. Let's communicate with them the way they want to be communicated with. Why do we have to call them all the time?"

Handal of Jim Koons says that texting is "the second-best new technology that has really helped," with multi-point inspection (MPI) software being Number One.

"Texting has really helped us communicate with the customer. It needs to be integrated. Customers love it."

Overall, says Donnie Pelkey, director of service operations for Fowler Auto Group, "Communication is critical to vehicle owners."

"Everyone is busy and doesn't want to wonder what's going to happen with their vehicle," says Pelkey, whose employer has seven dealerships representing nine brands in Denver, Oklahoma City and Tulsa.

That's why communicating with your employees, and technology-enhanced communications among your employees, is critical: How else can they communicate effectively with customers?"

And one more thing: Service departments must be able to create a true partnership with their technology vendors, or the entire installation—and attempt to leverage software to provide a customer-centric dealership—is imperiled.

"There's no way for the dealership to be experts across all their software packages, so a real vendor partnership is critical to success," Pelkey says.

"We can't be the software experts and know everything about all the products—not just features but reports and what they mean. There are just too many."

## The Inner Circle

With our preview of the Outer Circle of primary components of the customer-centric dealership, let's drill into the Inner Circle of secondary components. Each is important in its own way, and the Outer Circle components complement the Inner Circle building blocks.

## Scheduling

Scheduling is the first stage of the overall service experience, and when done properly, it can be one of the main drivers of a technology-enhanced experience.

How do you make that happen? You can load the shop very tightly using scheduling, optimizing capacity and driving key elements of the experience, while shrinking the write-up time because you're prepared with a thorough appointment.

You can enhance customer convenience through multichannel scheduling options: The customer can schedule by phone, computer or mobile device 24/7, from anywhere on the planet.

You provide professional and consistent menu recommendations and pricing through your scheduling system. Your appointment system can offer scheduling of transportation options such as rental or loaner cars, shuttle buses or Uber/Lyft.

Finally, powerful integration with recalls, declined services and promotions specific to that customer further enhance the overall scheduling experience.

## Marketing

You can have the best people, processes and in the area, but if you don't have a good service-marketing tool to let new customers know about you, and a robust way to communicate customer touch points, you're missing an important piece of being customer-centric.

Marketing is the "voice" of your technology-enhanced experience. Your marketing should be multichannel, personalized to the consumer and their vehicle, and your messages should have context and relevance.

Since your marketing communications should be the gateway into your service experience, deep integrations are a must-have.

### Service Advertising
Fixed Ops now contributes as much to profit as Sales

● Vehicle Sales ● Fixed Ops

| 5% | 12% | 49% |

| Service Advertising % | Fixed Ops Revenue | Gross Profit |

| Source: AmplifyRPM | Source: NADA | Source: NADA |

We should also consider how much we invest in service marketing. I advocate increasing your current spend to 15 percent of overall dealership advertising, so that you have a balanced service-marketing portfolio across search marketing, social media, and other channels in addition to your direct marketing.

A recent KBB study found that 29 percent of website visitors go to your service page, so ensure that at the center of your advertising is your dealership's website (or relevant social-media page). This is where specific landing pages and your service department pages help convert customers who are interested in service work into real opportunity.

## Training

New and remedial training for dealership employees is critical to achieving and maintaining customer-centricity. Training improves employee performance by providing your staff better understanding of their responsibilities in their role, and that also builds confidence.

Most people have gaps in their work skills. Regular training allows you to strengthen skills that need improving to elevate all employees to a higher level of skills, which also improves consistency.

And there are benefits to training that go beyond the customer: Providing training lets employees know that you're investing in them, which improves morale and therefore employee satisfaction. This in turn reduces employee churn, which is a significant problem for dealers these days, both in terms of the dollar expense and the degradation of the customer experience.

Finally, a training program provides a common set of concepts that employees can use as a springboard for additional suggestions and ideas on how to improve the customer experience.

## Processes

The person considered to be the father of total quality management (TQM), W. Edwards Deming, said it best: "A bad system will beat a good person every time."

For our purposes, a system is a set of processes and a process is a collection of related, structured tasks performed by people or equipment that produces a service or product for a customer.

This is why it is so critical that once we have people, culture and technology in place, we layer on them well-thought out, customer-centric processes.

The best way to create good processes is to use the PDCA method: Plan—Do—Check—Act.

PLAN: Design a business process to deliver a result.

DO: Implement the process and measure its performance.

CHECK: Evaluate the measurements relative to the desired result.

ACT: Decide on changes needed to improve the process. Focus on what the customer wants and needs and develop your processes around that.

## Key Takeaways:

- The model of a series of concentric circles is a good way to envision the building of a customer-centric enterprise.
- The Outer Circle of crucial components consists of Leadership, People, Capacity, Facilities and Technology.
- The Inner Circle of supporting elements consists of Scheduling, Marketing, Training and Processes.
- The inmost circle is made up of KPIs which indicate the state of the customer-centric experience at your dealership.
- All these elements work together to help you pivot toward a true customer-centric service department.

So now that we've established a model for a customer-centric dealership and taken an initial look at the primary elements in those rings, let's examine how you can put these into play as you set the stage for your relationship with future service customers—during the sale of the new or used vehicle.

# Chapter 5

## Secure the Handoff

There's a little technique that the best quarterbacks, and the best service managers, both practice: good handoffs.

And while Tom Brady or Aaron Rodgers may be handing the football to a running back for any number of reasons, there's no doubt about the purpose of handoffs in the auto-dealership environment: A handoff should set the stage for your future relationship with the customer in your service department.

I'm examining the handoff here because it is one of the simplest ways that dealerships can institute and demonstrate a new approach that puts the customer first.

Or think about it this way: If your dealership can't execute something as basic as the handoff and get it working in your favor, then you might not be ready to do most of the other things that are required to build a customer-centric operating philosophy.

It's uncomplicated, but vital, because it demonstrates a dealership's understanding of the fundamentals of building that customer-centric approach and of putting the customer at the center of everything.

The handoff doesn't need to involve digital technology or really any significant resource demands on the dealership at all. It's more a reflection of a commitment to customer-centrism, of a philosophy and a state of mind. And so, if you can get the handoff right, you've probably taken another step toward becoming customer-centric in many other areas of the enterprise.

But while the handoff is certainly something that most consumers will welcome, it's forgotten, ignored or overlooked at many dealerships. The dealers and their service leaders treat it as either an unimportant process or something that they don't want to impose on a customer because it takes a few minutes, or there's an underlying belief that the level of coordination needed between variable and fixed operations is too much to attain.

But think of it, again, from the customer's point of view: They went to your dealership to buy a vehicle and to experience a comprehensive transaction that, they hope, will answer all their questions about what they need to do for the ownership of their new vehicle. They'd prefer you be their one-stop shop.

I think that perhaps in some situations we've over-complicated what we think needs to happen in the sales-to-service handoff. We may think that it needs to be a big production—that may be one of the things holding us back.

We don't need to put on a pageant; there's plenty of downtime during the purchase of a vehicle. During one of those lulls, you can execute a handoff like this: Lead the customer over to the door into the service drive or department, open it and say, "And here's where you'll come for your first service visit. Here's the service drive where you pull in. There's Jane—hey Jane, here's Joe, a new customer!"

That's it. You don't need a big production; it can be as simple as that.

Customers don't want to have an experience with one person in sales that is completely disconnected from service, because they don't view their relationship with the dealership that way. They don't see or care about the invisible silos that separate variable from fixed operations; nor should they!

They bought this car from one dealer, and that showroom and that service department should all be part of one connected experience in their minds. That's how consumers want it.

Even better, the best practice is to help the vehicle-purchase customer set his first service appointment before he rolls that new vehicle out of the dealership. This is easily accomplished with most modern CRM systems at the push of a button. Check your CRM system to ensure it's integrated with service appointments.

By instituting the fundamentals of the handoff and setting the first service appointment, you'll lay the foundation for a significant improvement in retaining your vehicle-sales customers for subsequent service.

I play in a band sometimes, so I'll offer this analogy: Why would the audience want me to stand and plunk-plunk-plunk my bass without the other members of the band? They want an experience that is integrated, connected and seamless.

## The Power of a Positive First Impression

Getting that first appointment is key to establishing a service relationship, which may be the only opportunity you have to turn that person into a lifetime service customer. Research shows that you may see a 2.3-times increase in the return rate of customers when they are introduced to the service department at the time of purchase.[4]

And it's interesting that our industry is still having a lot of difficulty getting this concept—or at least the execution—right. In fact, over the last 20 years, we've spent tens of millions of dollars on consulting and training trying to do this correctly.

Yet the last research I saw showed only 41 percent of consumers recall being introduced to the service manager or a service advisor after they bought a car.[5]

**41%** were introduced to the service department at the time of purchase

Oddly enough, when I'm speaking to groups of service professionals and I ask how many work at a dealership that practices consistent sales-to-service handoffs, only about 5 percent of them say their dealerships are doing it consistently.

It's as basic as squeezing out a little bit of time during a vehicle-delivery process that still is interminably long, with lots of down time as the buyer waits for the financing process to be finished or waits, watching, while someone is vacuuming the floor mats.

The handoff should be one of the fundamentals of marketing our service department. It's something that dealers should be doing systematically, because it's their one, best opportunity to market future service to an "existing" customer.

[4] Source: Xtime 2017 Market Research
[5] Source: Cox Automotive Maintenance and Repair Study 2016.

## Target-Rich Environment

There's no better opportunity than people who are already feeling good about your dealership because they just agreed to make one of the biggest purchases of their lives from you, and it's all fresh and new.

Temecula Hyundai is one dealership that understands the importance of this opportunity and tries to take full advantage of it. They offer what Nicholson calls the "cook's tour" of the service department to new-car buyers and even to people who are shopping on the sales side of the dealership.

The success of this bit of marketing starts with determination and attitude.

"When you're building value in the dealership, you need to show them the full Monty," Nicholson says. "You need to show them what we have. And when you bring them to the back and show them your service department, how nice and clean it is, how nice your service writers are, you let the customer know just how friendly it is here.

"You say, 'Yeah, this is Steve, this is Travis, this is Carlos, this is Amanda, and you call everybody by their first name.

---
### *A real leader leads.*
---

"And then we walk them through the shop. We take them over to the early-bird [appointment] envelopes and show them how to do an early bird. And they might say, 'Wait a minute—I haven't even bought my car here yet.' And you say, 'Yeah—but you will! And when you do, we want you to know everything about our service department, because they are really good.'

"Even if I see a salesman on the lot who's struggling with a customer or hasn't done what he's supposed to do, what do I do? What does a real leader do? A real leader leads. And that's when I go over, and I get involved in that transaction. I tell the customer, 'Come on back here; I want to show you something.'

"You don't tell them that you want to take them to the service department, because they go, 'Oh, no, I don't need to see that.' I say,

'Come on, you've got to see this.' And then we take them in the back like it's something spectacular—because it really is."

Giving sales customers the cook's tour isn't the only thing Temecula Hyundai does to hand off these valuable customers to the service department, of course. The dealership also calls all its sales customers from the previous day and welcomes them to the Temecula family. The service manager further sends out a welcome -mail message to these folks and tries to go ahead and set their first appointment.

If they haven't gotten the quick tour when they were in the process of buying the vehicle, customers are asked when they come in for that first appointment if they want a look-around.

Using this approach, Nicholson says, Temecula has been able to offer a tour of its service department to about 75 percent of its sales customers over the last few years.

## Putting Money Behind Handoffs

Vaden Automotive Group is more assertive about the need for a handoff from sales to service. The salespeople include a service-handoff form in each vehicle purchase; each month, all the exceptions for deals that don't have a sign-off sheet are reviewed with the sales consultants.

"It's typically around 90 percent of our customers who get introduced to service in some facet," says Dawn Newsome, vice president of fixed operations for the enterprise that is headquartered in Savannah, GA. Vaden has 10 dealerships around Georgia, South Carolina and Alabama, including Chevrolet, Toyota and Nissan stores.

Salespeople either walk the customer back to the service department, even if it's after hours, or get a service advisor or manager to sign off on the sheet. Vaden's call-center personnel follow up with the customer to see if they have any questions about the car—and to set the first tentative service appointment.

There are lots of ways to make the handoff an effective marketing tool, and plenty of opportunity built into the sales process for determined service managers to make it work for their operations.

## Take Advantage of Technology

Every time a colleague or friend tells me about a recent vehicle purchase I'll ask two questions—"Do you know how to use all of the technology?" and "How did you learn how to use it?"

Invariably, most don't know much beyond the two or three cool things a sales associate pointed out. Others, who identified themselves as somewhat tech-savvy, almost always mentioned spending time with the owner's manual or looking up a new dashboard icon online.

These scenarios suggest opportunity to make sales-to-service handoffs, and initial service visits, more meaningful.

Let's remember, the technology-based bells and whistles matter to most of today's buyers. It seems wise to ease a likely uncertainty for some buyers that they're buying a lot of neat features that they may never use.

Your service department could be right there at the time of closing to reassure buyers: "After you've driven it for a while, if you're feeling unsure about how to operate this automated-safety or infotainment feature you just bought, contact us.

"It might comfort you a little bit to know that we have factory-authorized and factory-trained technicians here whose job it is to understand exactly how these complex new systems operate, and we have genuine factory parts that work best in your vehicle.

"And, by the way, let me show you where our service department is, how easy it is to get in to see us, and meet some of our friendly staff."

All of this means that it's even more important for building a customer-centric dealership that customers are shown the service department after they're handed the keys to their new vehicle.

This likely requires a new type of choreography between variable and fixed operations, but whatever investment in people and time that requires, it's worthwhile.

**Key Takeaways:**

- The handoff of a customer after their purchase of a new vehicle is a simple exercise but is often neglected.
- Done right, the handoff can be a highly effective way to introduce the service department and, in the process, to boost customers' good feelings about the entire dealership.
- To execute the handoff effectively, both variable and fixed operations need to commit to the principle and to set up processes to ensure that it's done effectively.
- Set the first service appointment in conjunction with the handoff.
- Ensure pay plans are aligned to drive the desired behavior.

# Chapter 6
Bringing Tech-Minded Customers
to Your Service Department

I had the opportunity to reminisce with a Cox Automotive colleague who's been going to NADA conventions for 50 years.

He was a kid back in 1969, when he attended his first convention with his dad, a Buick and Opel dealer.

He saved the program, and I found it fascinating.

For the roughly two days of meetings and workshops, there were only two sessions on technology, and both were basically about the availability and advancements in accounting systems.

We're a long way from there today. I know, if you're a dealer or service leader, there isn't a day that goes by that you don't receive a call or other communication about a technology solution that will help you in fixed operations.

At NADA, there are dozens of different solutions and providers. It's dizzying, sometimes, to know, exactly, where to begin.

From my conversations, the best place to start applying technology to drive a customer-centric experience in your service department is scheduling.

It's there you have an initial touch point that gives you the opportunity to convey, "We're tech-smart, and know you like to manage your service appointment and commitment."

Vaden Automotive Group understood this shift in customer expectations, and the benefits a technology-enhanced experience would provide back in 2012.

Vice President of Fixed Operations Newsome, who oversees 30 service advisors and roughly 65 technicians, remembers the early days, when she purchased scheduling software and stopped using the scheduling function in the company's Dealership Management System.

Her recollections about that period are instructive for dealers and service leaders today who are faced with big decisions about how to make sure their store gets customer-centric before the competition, and how to use technology to help make the critical transition.

Newsome's feelings about the transition seven years ago mirror those I hear from her peers today: It's time to do it. But it's going to take time to do it right.

She understood that once the dealership made the decision to use new digital platforms to transform the service operation and create a truly customer-centric experience, the first step was going to have to be scheduling software. It's how to get customers into the building in the first place. She also made sure the software properly connected to write-up tools for service advisors and customers to ensure a seamless experience from scheduling to the service visit.

She knew she would face resistance internally. "In the car business, we like instant gratification," Newsome says. "So, most often, when something doesn't work on day one or day two, we tend to abandon it and go with either what we know, or what's comfortable, or what we think is going to produce instant results.

"But I saw the writing on the wall very quickly as far as where the market was heading with quick service and maintenance, versus repair. I knew if we didn't have a very specific process, a very specific tool to measure our effectiveness with quick service and maintenance, we wouldn't be able to survive. It was crucial to get those tools in place."

Still, Newsome tells me, creating broad adoption across Vaden

and its many dealerships took sticks as well as carrots.

"The biggest thing was that we stuck with it and kept pushing on our people. I tied pay plans to it. We started out tying our tablet utilization to individual pay plans. Then it was their use of [scheduling software], their ASR [additional service recommendations] percentage, their inspection percentage, it was their closing percentage. So, a lot of their pay plans and their bonus levels are driven by their achievement of those goals.

"And in certain stores, I had penalties in place. If we fall below 85 percent utilization of the tablet, advisors participate financially. If they're at 85 percent or above, there's no extra pay, no bonus. I did that because that's part of their job. I didn't necessarily want to bonus them for doing what they were supposed to do, but I penalized them for not doing the bare minimum.

"And then on the [inspection] side of it, they get bonuses of around 25 percent to 30 percent of their pay that is based in part around their metrics on the system."

Indeed, Newsome says that it wasn't long before Vaden's service writers and technicians understood what their fixed-operations leader was doing, and why. "We talked about it every week, on every fixed call that we had," she recalls. "It became an everyday part of my life. There were some growing pains. It didn't happen overnight, but we are at the top of our game right now. It's really paid off.

"And now we're at a 70-to-30 ratio of customer-pay quick service to repair. And about 85 percent of our people who were with us stayed with us over time."

Meanwhile, Vaden's service retention hovers around 67 percent, and over the last year its customer pay increased by 15 percent to 20 percent.

---

*Tying pay plans to performance can be a key tactic. As my first mentor used to tell me, "If you want to understand why someone in business behaves the way they do, just read their pay plan."*

---

## A Critical Stage-Setter

Starting your technology strategy with scheduling offers another benefit: If you're going to do it *properly*, first you must take complete stock of your service operation—the number of techs, bays, hours of operation, advisors, equipment. Also, you have to ask how you plan to sell, use menus, pricing transportation options, and more.

It can seem a time-consuming, even mind-numbing exercise. But it's super-critical to ensure your technology investment fits the customer-centric operation you've chosen to create. This early work also helps you gain deeper familiarity and understanding of your operation, and it helps you envision the stages of different technology adoption you'll want to make along the way to becoming customer-centric.

It shouldn't matter if customers are initiating contact with your dealership in response to a marketing e-mail, because they hear a rattle under the hood, or because they're following the manufacturer's instructions on routine maintenance, you've got to have a platform that both captures that customer's outreach and commences an experience with your dealership that is complete, smooth and satisfying from the first interaction.

Customers should be able to make appointments easily online, from their laptop, home computer, or from their smartphone. And they should still be able to make that traditional phone call to set up a service appointment.

## Two Experiences

At Koons Ford-Lincoln-Mazda in Maryland, Fixed Operations Director Ruprecht has taken this approach to scheduling and has found that 35 percent of appointments now get scheduled online because it's easy for customers to make the appointment; that's about double the national average rate and compares with only 6 percent to 7 percent online reservations about five years ago at the dealership—a huge improvement.

*"35 percent of appointments now are scheduled online because it's easy for customers to make the appointment."*

"Our target is to get the customer on and off our [online] scheduler with an appointment in less than two minutes," Ruprecht tells me. "And if they make a phone call, to get them off the phone within three minutes with an appointment."

Marno Muth relocated from the Washington, D.C. area to become service manager at Hilton Head Honda, a single-rooftop store with a deep presence in the tourist town. Hilton Head Honda has four service advisors, 10 technicians and 14 service bays.

And when he arrived at the dealership about two years ago, Muth was determined to get the dealer up to speed with scheduling software as his top priority. He knew it would be critical if he expected the dealership's break to a customer-centric operating philosophy to succeed.

"Before I even physically stepped foot in the door to start my first day, I was in Virginia configuring it from afar—setting up teams, setting up schedules, and so forth," Muth recalls.

He also knew that the dealership overall would benefit as much as the consumer. "I don't think customers really see the difference in terms of what we do on the scheduling side," Muth tells me. "They might see us with the tablet, greeting them in the lane. Of course, they do see it when they're scheduling an appointment online as well.

"But on the back end, I feel it's more of a tool for me and my team. I think we see it more than [customers]. At the end of the day, the result that we yield from using everything together—our management team sees it; our owner sees it. It definitely has helped the bottom line."

Thus, as Muth tells it, Hilton Head Honda's appointment rate online is about 12 percent and "I would love to see that hit 20 to 30 percent over time. I think it can get there.

Think about what it would mean for your business if 30 percent or more of your customers made their service appointments themselves. The benefits, in my view are pretty rich: fewer customers calling, fewer customers taking our time on phone lines, fewer customers calling and not getting through and calling our call center—which charges by the minute.

"So instead they get to deal directly with our scheduling software, and they can see the same schedule that we do. There's no delay in terms of how many days they're allowed to book ahead of time. Providing that convenience for them is one of the biggest things."

Muth says that one obstacle he confronted both at his previous post, at a large dealership group, and at Hilton Head Honda is that it's difficult for dealership employees, especially those in service, to automatically understand customers' frustrations with scheduling because they don't go through the experience. They drop off their car when they get to work, and it's done when they need to go home.

"They really don't understand what it's like for customers," Muth says. "So, I have to tell them, 'Hey, how would you feel if you went to a restaurant and they told you it would take two hours without an appointment?' Of course, the restaurant will work you in, and so do we. But, next time you go, you make a reservation. You prepare ahead."

## Say Goodbye to The Morning Rush

Among other major advances for the dealership, scheduling software

solves one of the industry's biggest challenges: Everyone seems to want to get their vehicles in the shop first thing in the morning.

"You walk into any service department and ask them, 'Hey, when is your busiest time?'" Muth observes. "They're going to tell you that it's 8, 9, maybe 10 in the morning—first thing in the morning. And you look at the physical layout of the service lane, and if it's a small dealer, the lanes may hold only four or five cars at a given time.

"You walk in and look at what's going on without [scheduling software] and you see that there are cars backed up. Cars, tires sitting outside of the lane and hung outside, or whatever. And cars that are coming in all at the same time because everyone wants to come in at 8 or 9."

Hilton Head Honda had its own morning "service rush" issues. For starters, it's a small dealership, servicing a relatively small city. Then there's the extra logistical complication of the spring-through-fall tourism season.

"Everyone in our town wants to come in ASAP, and get everything done, and beat the tourism traffic back home," Muth explains. "Typically, that's before noon. In the very beginning, of course everyone would request an early time slot and there was pushback when we would say, 'I'm sorry, we don't have 8:30 available. We're fully booked, but I can accommodate you at a different time.' And I feel like in the beginning it was a little bit difficult for our advisors to counter that.

"That was a problem, and (our DMS) system didn't have a measure in place to limit how many appointments you can have at a given time. Everyone just books it based on what the customer wants or what they want. All the cars are coming in at the same time and you're getting crushed by everyone arriving at the same time."

Yet, Hilton Head Honda's problem is very similar to morning rushes that occur all over the United States for reasons that might vary locally but add up to the same basic challenge.

"The solution is [scheduling software]," Muth insists. "You set up the appointments, then you can set up to limit waits at a certain time. You can spread everyone out, and you can stagger appointment slots. And that's exactly what I did. And immediately when I implemented that, the advisors saw the benefit and value behind it.

"And if they're disciplined, they stick with it—they don't force appointments. That might be the biggest selling point for my advisors in terms of using scheduling and adapting to it and not fighting it."

Even once the scheduling software automatically distributed appointments efficiently, some service advisors still fought the technology, Muth says.

"Rather than saying, 'Oh, just come on in, we'll make it work,' I think over time they got better at saying, 'Oh, we're fully committed with this schedule, but how does 10:30 sound? Or if you want to come in at a quieter time, 2:30, you'll be in and out within 30 minutes or 45 minutes.'

"Whereas in the morning, a lot of times you'll hear advisors say that the schedule is fully booked. We accept walk-ins, but the wait is 45 minutes to two hours or three hours. And we have to be realistic with that because that's the truth. So now we've got better pushback for customers who want a particular slot."

Scheduling software should help the service department overall by reserving time for a certain number of walk-ins, in addition to your appointment customers.

The software should be able to segment appointment and non-appointment customers and give you enough control over shop scheduling that it can handle the usually predictable incidence of walk-in customers—and warn you when things have gotten out of whack.

A really good way to make sure walk-in experiences don't go off the rails is to offer a be-back coupon to customers when you can't fit them in that day, to optimize the chances of them returning to your service department.

### Key Takeaway:

- Scheduling is the initial touchpoint of your technology-enhanced experience.
- Configure your scheduling system so customers can create a complete service appointment.
- Tell your customers they can schedule online - almost half don't know they can.

# Chapter 7

## A Low-Tech, High-Value Touch Point

While we're walking through the ways technology can help you create a customer-centric experience, it's worth noting an idea I'm hearing more about—a pleasant, human touch to greet customers when they drop off their vehicles.

The greeting isn't necessarily coming from advisors, but from someone with the right personality and presence to help customers feel comfortable. The greeting complements the easy, efficient, technology-driven scheduling experience. The greeting sets the stage for an understanding, even empathetic, and satisfying experience for them under the roof of your service department.

Customers should be greeted by someone almost immediately and their presence acknowledged, even if you can't get a service advisor in front of them just quite yet.

Jim Coleman suggests retirees and young people for the greeter job.

If he were opening a dealership right now, Coleman says, he would definitely hire greeters for the service lane. They would take over some of the face time now occupied by traditional service advisors, particularly by service advisors who aren't strong on empathy. They could be retirees like the senior-citizen greeters traditionally employed by Walmart's, or maybe younger people who serve as greeters at Apple's Genius Bar locations.

"These would be friendly, non-aggressive people who would walk the car with the customer," Coleman says. "Then the greeter would hand off the customer to a clerical person who would process and print the RO, similar to call-center agents who require less training because they do things exactly the same way every time. You could replace service advisors with non-aggressive people who make suggestions.

"How many retired people would like to have something to do for three or four hours each morning? I think it would improve processes for both service advisors and managers. It's a great and inexpensive way to improve your customer relationships.

Temecula Hyundai staffs the service drive each day with two young people who serve as greeters. Within two to three minutes of a service customer approaching the department, one of them greets the customer with their  tablet and immediately begins the check-in process.

"That is clutch," Nicholson says. "If a customer is waiting and waiting and no one is talking to them, you've already lost them."

These greeters also offer customers a cup of coffee or a bottle of water as soon as they enter the service drive. "It's all part of lean thinking," Nicholson says. "Let's not send customers on a goose chase to go get something they want. That way, I can keep them right in the service drive while we complete the write-up process."

OK. Enough of the low-tech stuff. Let's get back to how technology itself can help you create a customer-centric experience.

# Chapter 8

Bringing Technology to The Lanes

Let's start by unpacking the significance of the tablet computer using a digital engagement platform in the early stages of the service experience.

In the service lane, a true customer-centric experience requires the de-tethering of service advisors from their worn-down swivel chairs and desks. This typical set-up doesn't allow a more active welcoming and evaluation process for the customer that fits their expectations of the service visit. Mobile devices powered by the right software solve this all-too-common problem.

At Hilton Head Honda, Muth says that advisors "always have their iPads in their hands when they're out in the lane. We don't have clipboards in sight. I don't even know where to find them anymore.

"You feel naked without the tablet nowadays. They're charged in my office [overnight] and the guys grab them every morning, and sometimes they panic if the battery is dead or something.

"If for some reason they don't have one, they're lost; it's a tool. And a clipboard isn't really a tool anymore; it's just a writing platform. It's not offering anything beyond that.

"This industry is really antiquated, and [use of iPads in the service lane] is one of the first steps to introduce technology in a simple way. It's a very simple approach to do a presentation with tablets. And I think we'll start catching up our technology use with other industries now."

The leader of a large midwestern dealer group talks about his transition to a technology-driven service lane with a dose of humor.

"Every time I would ask a customer to go through a check-in using the iPad, I never once had somebody tell me they would prefer the old way of doing business" with clipboards, the leader of the large midwestern dealer group says. "It's just a matter of getting our employees to do it long enough to kind of realize that."

From my conversations with dealers, I've gleaned a few lessons learned to help you successfully adopting service lane technology:

**Lesson 1: Ensuring its proper integration with your DMS. Consider the experience of Jim Koons Automotive Group.**

The company has 124 service advisors and many years ago spent more than $150,000 on tablets to bring them to its service lanes. But they encountered a big problem—the tablets didn't work with the DMS.

"A few months into it, I found out the advisors didn't like using the tablets because it took them longer than using paper," says Handal, vice president of fixed operations for Koons "I tried using them only in the express lane but got the same results.

"We pulled them out completely, waited for the integrations to be improved, then re-launched" when the company began implementing new engagement software. "Now it's much faster and it's doing great. The lesson for us was if the technology isn't going to save time, service advisors won't use it."

**Lesson 2: Dedicate yourself to encouraging and enforcing tablet use once you've implemented them. Given the chance, some service advisors will still ditch them in favor of those old clipboards.**

At Temecula Hyundai, for instance, Nicholson had to dedicate much of his first day on the job to getting service writers re-aligned with their iPads. He found the tablets where his predecessor had left them: in a drawer in his office, out of power and about three software updates behind. No way were they going to work in that condition.

**Lesson 3: Get your people to define (and refine) your tablet process.**

Your advisors are in the trenches, the tablets are in their hands. They often can be the best resource for figuring out the most efficient way to employ tablets and technology as part of your engagement process.

"We put it in their hands and turn a couple of guys loose on it and say, 'Hey, tell us what's good and what's bad,'" says Vince Sweeney, a director of fixed operations for Fletcher Jones, a luxury-car dealer with stores in California, Hawaii, Nevada and Illinois.

"We let them actually build our internal process. We knew what we wanted, but we kind of let them give us feedback to drive us to what we were trying to accomplish. And eventually their buy-in came and now you just see them picking up, grabbing their tag and walking to the car with their tablet under their arm. Every time now—I mean, it's without exception.

"And they're around the car, and they're marking things down, they're checking damage. And it works very, very well. So, overcoming those obstacles to the buy-in was the biggest thing, but letting them steer the ship was really what made it work."

## Lesson 4: Make sure your infrastructure is sound.

As dealerships move to tablet-based check-ins, they often encounter another obstacle: inadequate infrastructure for the devices to work.

This is a case of where dealers need to reinforce an important structural element in their Outer Circle, Facilities, to ensure that an important component of the Inner Circle, Processes, also helps create a customer-centric dealership experience.

At Temecula Hyundai, for example, once Nicholson got the dealership's iPads powered up and digitally updated, he found that weak Wi-Fi was disabling them. He persuaded the dealership principal to invest $3,800 to put in a Wi-Fi system that was dedicated only to writing service.

This is a very important and often overlooked point when implementing new, mobile technology. You've got to be rock solid in accessing your network, or your new tech could die a quick death. Slow or intermittent access will aggravate customers and employees alike. Check it out and invest as necessary.

"This piggy-backing we'd done off the Wi-Fi for the customer lounge –it didn't work," Nicholson recalls. "That dog wasn't going to hunt. And what I needed to do as an administrator, as a leader, was to eliminate all the excuses that [service writers] could possibly come up with as to why they wouldn't buy into the tablets."

Even more, Temecula Hyundai installed a booster antenna on the front of the dealership that would service the iPads from the very front of the lot to the very back, about 100 yards in all.

"I want to be able to write service all the way out to the end of our property, so at the end of the day, I've eliminated the excuse for even the slowest writer in the line, that he doesn't have Wi-Fi and that the iPad won't work," Nicholson says. "That's when it became fun, too, because I could say to the service advisors, 'Don't you love this thing?'"

## Lesson 5: Use the technology to its fullest.

Once the use of tablets and engagement software by service advisors is routine, service departments can benefit in tangential ways that they don't typically foresee.

For instance, at Temecula Hyundai, one service writer experienced an "Aha!" moment when he led a walk-around of a car with the owner and took the standard photographs that are required by the software, even though the car was in for mechanical, not cosmetic, service.

"The [spouse] comes to pick up the car in the evening, looks at it and says, 'You dirty, rotten SOBs, look at the scratches that are on that car'" Nicholson recalls.

"But the service writer says to himself, 'Aha!,' opens up the iPad and shows the person the pre-existing scratches from the photos in the inspection. And the person's face went blood-red, then pale—they were so embarrassed. But that's all it took for that service writer to become a big believer in the software."

## Lesson 6: Make transparency a priority.

A truly customer-centric experience doesn't hide or shade the truth. It embraces it. Why? Because it sets the correct expectation with customers that you're on their side, and you care about their cars.

Service-lane technology helps you advance a customer's trust by making it easy to present all the potentially relevant routine maintenance services they made need.

"We always present a menu to someone who comes in the door," says Williams. "Whether the car has one mile or four billion miles.

Here's why: When you show the menu for $99.95, now customers know the price. So next time, there's no shock and awe. And you build honesty and integrity right in the driveway.

"And then every time a customer comes in, they're going to feel a little sense that people are taking care of them because we're doing the same process we do every time."

Also crucial: What is offered on the menu. Customers need to be assured that the last thing you're trying to do is take advantage of them. If they come to think the latter, even with something like a menu listing, you may have lost them for good.

Ensure menu items are explained as factory recommendations, or as dealer-recommended with a very clear explanation as to why the recommendation solves an immediate and understandable problem.

Koons, for example, sticks with the factory recommendations and doesn't add additional services to its menu.

"If the factory says in the owner's manual, 'It needs an air filter at 30,000 miles service,' that's all the car is going to get," says Ruprecht, the fixed-operations director for the three-brand dealership. "If the client comes in and we inspect the fluids, and the fluid is dirty, and it needs replacement or exchange, we will tell him, 'You need an exchange based on what we see here.'

"But if the factory says, 'The 30-000-mile service includes an oil change, tire rotation and replace the PCV valve or air filter,' that's what we sell them when we come in.

"We don't over-recommend, so we set our recommendations to average recommendations. We target two to three recommendations per RO, and then set a goal of closing half of them. If you do close 50 percent, you're golden. Then I can tell you we have great and ethical sales per repair order.

"And the experience for our customers is to make sure we're recommending what the cars need in service—not to over-recommend and to over-sell. That's the biggest factor for the dealership-retention issue."

## Lesson 7: Keep your promises.

If a customer is waiting on premises or off, your system must be able to give them an accurate promise time.

Then you've got to provide that customer with a regular update, preferably about halfway between when you promised the vehicle and the drop-off: If you promised the vehicle four hours from when the customer brought it in, contact them at the two-hour mark.

There isn't any particular research to support the idea that you should give this notice at about the halfway point; it just makes sense. Halfway through what they thought the time duration would be, most customers still aren't anxious about how it's going, still aren't particularly concerned because they haven't heard from you. And yet once they do, they can kick back with the assurance that the appointment is running on time. This is the minimum you should do for updates.

The best practice is to use a system that automatically sends regular updates to all customers, utilizing their preferred communication channel. Regular notifications that confirm all is proceeding according to plan, or that inform the customer of a status change. You need to let them know immediately when a deviation becomes apparent, along with providing them a new promise time. Then your status update re-sets itself.

### Key Takeaways:

- Greeting the customer immediately is critical, setting the stage for their entire experience.
- Menu selling should be based on fair and transparent pricing and only include factory recommendations or items that solve an immediate and identifiable problem.
- Don't shirk on promise times; be transparent with customers and keep them informed.

# Chapter 9

Bringing Technology to Your Bays

I f there's one thing that generates debate among service leaders, it's about the effectiveness and efficacy of multi-point inspections (MPIs).

Some don't think MPIs are worth it at all. They believe the MPI reports are customer-killers: Who wants to see a laundry list of potential problems (and their price tags) when they only brought their vehicle in for an oil change?

Some also question if the extra work MPIs require of advisors and technicians is simply too much, given all the other competing demands and priorities. But others wouldn't run their customer-centric service departments any other way. For them, MPIs are a key part of their customer-centric operating philosophy. Each MPI report isn't an indictment of a vehicle, or a cause to ring the cash register, it's an attempt to build confidence and trust between you and the customer and, in some cases, between them and their vehicle.

As you might expect, I fall into this second camp. I've seen the power of a properly managed MPI process light up service departments across the country. The right MPI tools give you a track record of a vehicle's needed work, customer approvals or rejections, and a way to more efficiently manage internal workflows when the MPIs generate additional work.

I would add, however, that it's critically important that dealers not abuse the inspections function. To quote Carl Sewell, the Texas luxury-car megadealer who wrote a great book on the topic customer service, *Customers for Life*: "You can shear a sheep a hundred times, but you can only skin him once."

Let's look at how some dealers have made MPIs a critical cog in their efforts to deliver a customer-centric service experience—and how MPIs help their businesses.

"We adopted the service inspection before it was the popular word of the day," says Billy Monteverde, service director for Ferman, a two store Chevrolet-Volvo dealership in central Florida with about a half-dozen service advisors and 18 technicians.

"Checking batteries on the drive, interacting with the guest, checking light bulbs and, you know, tire-tread life and all your safety items. Doing a three-minute walk-around. It was nothing exotic, but we did it before it was popular per se."

For sure, there are ways to conduct multi-point inspections that actually adhere customers more closely to your dealership in a positive way—and that bolster the dealership's bottom line. The successful approaches involve a customer-communications proficiency, proper training of service-department employees, and, nowadays, a software platform that helps in both areas.

Scott, of Bob Johnson Chevrolet, believes that "the cool thing is you're going to get immediate results by using" inspection software to standardize and streamline this process. "You thought you were doing multi-point inspections, but your people really weren't. Nobody is who doesn't have a management system that's easy to work.

"The fact that you have a way of making sure everybody is doing a thorough multi-point inspection on every car and that you have a way of measuring and communicating closing rates with advisors—just those two things drive more business. Because frankly it's all the stuff you should have been doing but weren't."

Similarly, the multi-point-inspection procedure and software are paying off for a large midwestern dealer group: The company is now using inspection software for about 90 percent of vehicles that come into its service bays, well on its way to its goal of 95 percent. It has set an ASR goal of 45 percent, and many of the large midwestern dealer group stores have already reached that level.

Handal, of Jim Koons Automotive, which has nearly 500 technicians, provides one of the most robust endorsements of the importance of consistent multi-point inspections and software.

"The MPI was our Number One tool to improve the customer experience and increase sales," he says. "It pulled the service advisors, techs and parts people together and has been the biggest improvement as far as new technology goes.

"I've been watching it for eight years, and it's been the biggest factor. You can look at closings by service advisor, monitor low producers, see guys who are trying to over-sell—it's all in black and white and allows you to pinpoint issues much faster than versus the old, manual ways."

## Do It Right the First Time, Every Time

One of the advantages of using multi-point inspection systems is a consistent approach and process that guides the technician through the same inspection regimen every time.

Additionally, dealerships should perform these inspections even if they know they'll find absolutely no "red" items that demand attention or "yellow" ones that suggest it. Even if it's a brand-new car, inspect it—do it for your credibility. Customers should be able to expect an inspection every time they come in for service.

Another excuse I hear is that the car was just in a month ago—why inspect it again so soon? Well, no service advisor or technician that I know is clairvoyant. You have no idea how or where that vehicle has been driven. You never know when something might demand attention.

Doing an inspection first time, every time without exception shields the dealer from liability. If you inspect the vehicle when there's a good chance it doesn't need any work—selling the "green," as my friend Nicole Redding likes to say—the practice enhances your credibility for when you inspect the vehicle and you do find something. Plus, you make the customer feel good about their vehicle—and about you.

Consider this analogy: If I'm a dentist and you come in for an exam and you walk out with a clean bill of health, I have credibility with you that you're going to get the straight story the next time you come in for an appointment.

Same with a service department: If you only perform an inspection when it seems obvious the vehicle needs some attention, and then you can sell some extra parts or services, you're a dealer who's transparently transaction-centered and it seems that you're trying to optimize that transaction.

## Make Parts Part of Your MPI Plan

An additional consideration, the leader of the large midwestern dealer group notes, is that as you're implementing the multi-point inspection system, don't forget the parts manager. Dealing effectively with the parts operation can be one of the largely unseen, but most important, process in keeping customers at the center of the service department.

"It's very important to integrate the parts department with inspection because if a technician is trying to use something they're not happy about, and the job gets stuck in the parts department, it can be a train wreck," the leader of the large midwestern dealer group says.

"They have to be strong in the process. We didn't put enough emphasis on parts during the set-up and training aspect. It was kind of like, 'OK, here's everything in place and by the way, parts, you're involved in this one, too.'

"During the set-up phase I make sure both the service and parts manager are engaged. In the beginning we did not focus enough on the part department which caused some frustration during the rollout phase."

## Nudging the Nay-sayers

If you opt to implement an MPI process as part of your customer-centric operating philosophy, you'll run into resistance, as sure as the sun will rise tomorrow.

"You have to view this as an evolutionary process," says Ward of Summit Automotive. "Not everyone will come along at first."

Human beings are creatures of habit. So it's human nature to resist change, and it's harder for some to get over the hump when it's in front of them.

Therefore, when asking us to embrace and use new technology, it often requires new processes which can go against current habits.

Communication is key! You must ensure the associates understand how and why the technology will make their work lives easier, their customer's experience better and ultimately improve the dealership overall (in that order).

For these tools to work at maximum proficiency, it is important that all associates pull together as a single unit. Advisors, technicians, parts specialists, manager... everyone! As soon as one aspect of the team stops performing their tasks, it affects all others.

"Back in the old days, you would ask technicians to do multi-point inspections, and they would sort of try to do them," says the fixed-operations director for a large dealership group in Ohio with several rooftops, 25 service advisors and 60 technicians.

"And we would sort of try to track them in big paper stacks. And we'd have people filing them and trying to measure them and trying to figure out what an ASR was, and cashiers recapping things. We would do all of that and then what you would run into is that it was completely unmanageable because it was too much of a paper project; we couldn't keep up with it.

"And, number two, the technician had a very, very quick dodge if they had decided they didn't just feel like doing multi-point inspections or that they were wasting our time doing it, they wouldn't. They would say that nobody would sell any extra service work based on what their multi-point inspection found.

"But when we're on the performance review calls with our vendor and technicians hear about how much extra work we're closing with the multi-point inspection platform, they no longer have the excuse of saying, 'When I find work, nobody sells it.'

"And this is really the point—the almost silent point—of letting the inspection tool manage itself. It's almost a self-policing environment with peer pressure. And you have that third-party performance manager for the software telling us objectively how we've all performed."

And multi-point inspections, done right, can help create lifetime customers. "Here's a great example of how it looks when it starts to take hold: We're working in the service lane on a Friday and a customer walks in and he's dealing with one of our top service writers, Eric," recalls Sweeney.

"He says, 'Eric, you told me about these tires before. I'm due.' And Eric says, 'It's great that you're taking care of your car. We also noticed that your brakes are 'yellow.' You know what? Let's take a peek at them next time you come in. You'll probably be due.'

"It's just setting it up," concludes Sweeney. "And I think there's as much value in 'green' inspections as there is in closing an ASR today. It's the trust factor. We have to overcome that part of our business—that people don't trust us walking in.

"When you walk back and say, 'Hey, your 'A' service is done and everything on the car looks great,' the customer is, like, 'Hmm, OK—wow, maybe you guys aren't so bad.'"

Does that sound like Fletcher-Jones has created a customer for life? That's what the use of multi-point inspection software is all about.

### Key Takeaways:

- Inspection programs also are vital both for fully informing and pleasing the customer and for maximizing service departments' revenue potential.
- The parts department plays a vital role in ensuring that the dealership can perform any extra repairs or services in a timely manner.
- Resistance to change by technicians and/or advisors can be expected, so identify advisors/techs to lead the change, remind them of "WIFM," and be persistent.

While mobile devices, and engagement and inspection software don't comprise a silver bullet for a dealership that is on the wrong track, they can be effective pieces of an Inner Circle of tools and processes that surrounds the customer with attention and care and helps create a truly customer-centric experience.

# Chapter 10

Establishing a Customer-Centric Culture

F ew workplaces on earth may be as unfamiliar with change as an automotive dealership. And, OK, this includes the service departments of automotive dealerships.

Yet, these days, you'd be hard-pressed to find a business where transformation of the customer experience, and the accompanying need for sometimes-radical change, are more crucial. That calls for some drastic transformations of people, technology and culture in our dealerships.

To build a truly customer-centric experience, in fact, People and Culture may be the most important components of that Outer Circle. You can have all the physical presence you want, represented by capacity and facilities and technology in our Outer Circle.

But if you don't have the right people in place, from top to bottom, and they aren't acting within a culture where true customer-centrism is planned, enacted, studied and improved, you're not going to be able to get the customer to that crucial spot in the middle of those concentric circles.

Here are some steps for initiating a culture change in your dealership:

- Someone needs to step up and lead.
- Publish your customer-centric values to employees and customers.
- Begin hiring to reflect your customer-centric values.
- Train your employees (new and existing) to reflect your customer-centric values.
- Identify and celebrate customer champions.
- Adjust your metrics to be customer-centric.
- Adjust your pay plans to reflect your customer-centric values.
- Reinforce the culture daily, weekly and monthly in meetings, company newsletters, recognition from management and spot spiffs.

In automotive retail, one of the gold-standard dealer groups for culture is, of course, the Sewell Auto Group based in Texas. Over 100 years old and led by the fourth generation of the family, they currently have 19 rooftops.

Carl Sewell published *Customers for Life* in 1990, detailing his relentless focus on customer service. When you read the book and other interviews Sewell has given, his basic view of customers is that you should treat them as you want to be treated and create a culture that supports this approach, throughout your dealership or dealer group.[6]

To accomplish this, you must be laser-focused on hiring the right people, providing them training, and then constantly pushing them. If you hire correctly, you'll get performance but also retention—a large percentage of his team have worked for Sewell for decades.

When meeting with job candidates, they're told that they'll feel a hand in their back pushing them to get better always. If they're not comfortable with that, they should not take the job.

"It's always delivering a message of expectation that we need to perform at the very highest level," said Sewell, who oversees human-resources development for the dealership group still today.

This is a great example of the leader of the organization driving the culture, but it's not an isolated example. The owner of a large midwestern dealer group, holds company-wide, town-hall-style forums twice a year where non-management employees get the opportunity to tell him how the large midwestern dealer group is falling short in pleasing customers (OK, and employees, too) and to suggest how to remedy shortcomings.

"He's made it very clear for the entire organization that the customer is first," says the service leader of the large midwestern dealer group. "We all know his expectations. And to support that, we have vision and mission statements, core values that everyone is expected to adhere to. And if not, there's a fairly quick way out of the company."

With the culture and his expectations obvious, the owner of the large midwestern dealer group's people exercise the levers of recognition, evaluation and communication to reinforce the customer-centric credo of the company.

They conduct monthly and bimonthly reviews of everyone in the company, and in that process, it often picks up on employees who

[6] Sourced from Automotive News

deal well and maybe are going the extra mile for customers, as well as performers who might have good traditional stats but who don't seem to embrace a customer-centric approach.

To educate themselves about how service employees are performing in the consumer's eyes, the large group's managers e-mail a short survey to each customer quickly after a transaction—and well before they get any CSI survey from a manufacturer.

And what these tools say have consequences.

A case in point from 2018: the group dispatched a top service advisor to a dealership that was struggling with its CSI scores and obviously not satisfying customers. But within a few weeks after he arrived, a dozen positive surveys had come in from customers. The leader of the large midwestern dealer group took a clip of a very positive comment from one of the surveys and sent it to him.

"That was a struggling area of our company, and he made changes and updated some processes, so now this gentleman is getting positive reviews," the service leader of the group says. "We wanted him to know it's being noticed."

At the same time, both the customer surveys and management evaluations can yield some bad news for the dealer group's employees.

---

*We've lost people over that who are good performers on paper—but you have to do it the right way.*

---

"Things come out in those meetings that might show a guy selling 12 to 15 cars a month, or a service advisor writing $100,000 a month in sales, but not doing it the right way," the service leader says. "We've lost people over that who are good performers on paper—but you have to do it the right way.

"They're read by top management, and so they definitely know if there are trends in the dealership or with a certain employee who might consistently be getting bad reviews," the service leader says. "They make a point to correct the situation."

Darrel Ferguson shares a great example of how to lead change: a dealer he knows bought thousands of wiper blades in bulk, and then instructed his advisors to greet the customer in the drive and comment that their wipers looked worn.

At this point, the customer will be waiting for "I can replace those for only $25.

Instead the advisor says, "Let me replace those for you free while you tell me what you need."

What just happened? The entire dynamic of the discussion and the relationship changed. By offering this unexpected courtesy (which cost almost nothing, by the way), you've now built great credibility and trust and created a powerful moment for the customer. Will they be back? What do you think?

## Profiles in Customer-Centric Cultures

Another culture-minded dealer, who defines the culture at his dealership and also is walking the walk, is Ed Witt, principal of Witt Lincoln in San Diego.

In *Fast Lane*, I discussed some of the great customer experiences Witt and his team deliver, but this is more fundamental. His office opens out onto the service lanes, and I cannot count the number of times during a visit that Ed has suddenly stood up and said, "Be right back."

He had spotted something, maybe a customer looking lost or in need of help, and his reaction was always the same—*customer* first.

Ask yourself honestly: Do you and the people in your store have that attitude? If the answer is not a resounding yes, you've got some work to do.

I have a similar example from the Fred Beans Dealer Group headquartered in Doylestown, PA. They've been there for more than 50 years and now number 25 dealerships at 20 locations in Pennsylvania and New Jersey.

They are very focused on customer satisfaction and run all kinds of customer-centric programs, such as their AutoRewards loyalty platform. But more important is their cultural leadership.

A couple years ago, I was visiting Fred and his team at the Ford store in Doylestown. We'd had some good discussions and were going to dinner. It was winter in Pennsylvania, so it was cold, and it was nighttime.

I'm riding with Fred on the way to the restaurant. As we're driving by the Ford showroom, he *slams* on the brakes, throws it into park, blows his door open and disappears without a word. (Yes, I'm having a WTF moment at that point.)

I sit there for at least 10 minutes. Then, Beans returns, hops in, and apologizes for jumping out. He says, "I saw a customer in the showroom and no one was with her, so I needed to help her."

I've told that story about a hundred times, and the reaction is usually, "Wow!"

But when I told that story to a couple folks at Fred Beans, the reaction was, "And? ..." It's not remarkable to them at all.

That's because the culture at Fred Beans has been built around the customer for so long that it is firmly entrenched, and to the team there it is second nature—from the bottom to the top.

Gregg Manson is another veteran who has lived on the frontier of the cultural imperative in dealerships. For several years, he was the vice president of fixed operations for one of the largest dealer groups. . Part of this experience was in the Denver area, where he oversaw the cultural transformation of 22 service departments over eight years.

He had an approach for getting dealership employees to appreciate and embrace a customer-centric philosophy, and it started—almost literally—with forming a cross-function team of people to adopt the customer's point of view and follow the implications of that for their store.

"We would even hand out hats for them to wear that said, 'Customer,' on them," recalls Manson. "It just helped. They got the goal. It helped, because we literally wanted them to look at the store through customers' eyes."

Manson wanted the team members to adopt what the customer's perspective would be from the moment they drove onto the dealership's lot. What did they see? Can they figure out how to get to where they needed to go? If they knew nothing about the store, and had just bought a car from the dealership, what questions would they have?

As he repeated this exercise from shop to shop, Manson had to resist the temptation to supply his own answers, the ones he already knew were true from experience.

"I needed to turn it over to them and allow the team members to build the customer experience that they would want as a customer," Manson explains.

Inevitably, the teams' observations and conclusions broke down into a handful of buckets about how the service department could improve the customer experience.

One bucket was communications. When they drove their vehicle onto the dealership property, they wanted clear signage directing them to the service department.

Also, team members concluded that they should get immediate online confirmation that they'd made a service appointment, as in so many other types of commercial transactions. And they wanted to be able to communicate digitally with the dealership and not just via phone.

Engagement was another important area: When they arrived in the service drive, for instance, they expected to be greeted immediately and warmly—not necessarily written up immediately, but at least to have their presence acknowledged and an initial engagement take place.

A third bucket had to do with transparency. Inevitably, the teams would conclude that the customers wanted to know right away what they needed when they arrived for a service appointment, why they needed it, how much it would cost and when they would be able to get their vehicle back.

And so on. The point was that, after the team had been allowed to build their own expectations of a customer-centric experience for the dealership, they embraced their findings and expected them to be implemented. The team met regularly and shared their findings with other employees, mapping out a suggested process for implementing their recommendations by addressing gaps with signage, tools, processes and so on.

Once they were on board, of course, Manson says with a chuckle, "It was easier to hold them to what they had built than to what you built. Because these were their ideas, they were more likely to execute on them" and truly transform their operation into a customer-centric enterprise.

"And they were the ones sharing with everyone, 'This is where we are going,' rather than me telling everyone. At the end, that also allowed me to have everyone hold everyone else accountable for the changes."

By getting employees essentially to flesh out their own vision for a customer-centric service department, Manson also was helping to create an overall culture that would continue to put the customer first long after the team exercise had concluded and even after its recommendations were considered and implemented.

The process wasn't foolproof. In some instances, even management would get in the way. If they got wind of a team recommendation that seemed cockeyed, some managers couldn't hold back.

"If the team came up with something really off the wall, these managers would scoff at it and say they didn't want it; they wanted something else," Manson says.

"The problem with that was that they didn't allow the team to maybe fail and grow and then reflect back on what they were recommending. It should have been, 'OK, this didn't go as well as we wanted it to. How did that happen?' Allow the team to self-realize."

Another way that top management could interfere with this wonderful exercise in dealership transformation was subtler but just as dangerous: They didn't explicitly buy into what was going on.

So, implicitly, team members could feel somewhat insecure about participating. After all, while they were taking all this time away from their "day jobs" by participating on the team, they still had to avoid having a sub-par month.

"To avoid that, you need to get the clear buy-in of people not only at the manager level but at the owner-operator level," Manson says. "They need to understand that things didn't get broken overnight, so they're not going to be fixed overnight. And that they may have to sacrifice four hours a week out of some staff members, but that's an investment, and that's what is required to get to where we want to go.

"If the leadership above the service manager hasn't bought into this process, it'll never get off the ground."

Ferguson's experiences reinforce the lesson. "The biggest epiphanies always start at the top," he says. "They come back to the store with new tech, drop it and then wash their hands of it. Change really comes when the leaders/decision makers are engaged, or re-engaged, about changing people and culture to drive more customer-centric processes with a technology-enhanced experience.

"It's not just taking a paper form and making it electronic—it's deeper and harder than that. And it almost always has to come from the top, and until that light bulb goes on you don't see the necessary changes."

Of course, training your people is essential, not just in diagnostics and repair improvements for the techs but also for teaching customer-centric ways and underscoring their importance. Effective training is one of the best ways to build on the solid fundamentals of a customer-centric culture and a customer-centric workforce.

Notching some gains may be as simple as re-assessing the tasks managed by your service advisors. Former dealer and service operations executive for Ford, Jim Coleman, also sees a lot of shops where service advisors are inefficient and can do more in providing a customer-centric experience. Some advisors say they can only handle 10 to 12 customers per day—but he believes they're being vastly underutilized.

"I tell them, 'we're setting up a BDC, so if I take away all your phone calls and give you [an inspection tool], what are you really doing all day?" Coleman says. "The manager's assumption is that these guys are busy, but that's BS. If they check people in, it might take 10 minutes per; so, I'll give them 150 minutes a day for that.

"Dealing with texts is another 90 minutes, and that includes the follow-up they should be doing but aren't doing. So, yes, they've got time to do more, and we should expect more and hold them accountable—after all they're the primary interface with the customer so are the primary drivers of customer loyalty.

"Exacerbating the problem is managers aren't managing advisors, which is compounding the problems. 'People do what you inspect, not what you expect.'"

## Connecting Culture and Technology

To make cultural transformation thorough and enduring requires dealership leaders to be persistent and to nudge them continually in directions that ultimately lead to keeping the customer in the middle of those concentric circles around which the dealership is built.

But resistance to change among the rank-and-file, and often among managers, can be deep and stubborn.

Often the cultural resistance is expressed by rejection of technology that service departments introduce. Some personnel, especially tenured ones, simply won't embrace the digital technology and software systems on which the best service departments now run. They pose a challenge to building a customer-centric experience across the enterprise because they are just not used to thinking that way, a problem that manifests when they say "no thanks" to your investment in technology and tools to advance a customer-centric operating philosophy.

Some dealerships are fortunate in that software implementation goes smoothly and is eagerly embraced—or at least quietly accepted—by their service personnel.

At Hilton Head Honda, for instance, "I have a pretty good implementation here," Muth says. "We signed up; we implemented; and we used it. It was as simple as that. I didn't have too many challenges. I'm not sure why; I just feel lucky that my crew believed in me and the product and service, and they rolled with it without too much hesitation. Pretty much after their first day we were using tablets.

"A lot of service advisors: The factory tells them they have to do something, or the dealer principal tells them they have to do something. Or they do it grudgingly because they're hearing or seeing it everywhere else. And so, there are a lot of bumps under the carpet. Whereas, if you truly embrace it -- and I mean having genuine enthusiasm—that affects everybody else to some degree."

And there are ways to anticipate resistance and effectively undermine it before it even gets traction.

At Fox Motors, Turske looks for employees who might be "drivers" of technology change and ambassadors of a new platform to fellow workers.

"Without a doubt a big challenge was moving parts and service employees that are extremely busy and are comfortable in their day-to-day duties and asking them to significantly change how they do their job."

"And if something is already working for you and you're pretty successful at it, why change?

*"The biggest challenge was finding enough drivers of change. I needed to find change agents of the new system."*

"For me the biggest challenge was finding enough drivers of change. I needed to find change agents of the new system because there's no way I can do that at 20 or 25 stores; I can't be the driver. So, whenever we were getting ready to sign [a store onto the new platform], I would meet with the general manager and service manager, and I would say, 'Who's driving this system? Because it can't be me. I'm here to support you, but I can't be the driver.'

"I needed someone to take the reins in the dealership when I wasn't there. To be the cheerleader, too, because sometimes things don't always work right out of the gate when you're doing a major change like this. We just had to identify enough of those leaders to not say, 'Here's why we can't use the system,' but, 'Here's what we need to do differently to make the system work.'

"Since I could not be onsite for every store launch it was important to find enough store leaders to drive change. Even with the strong onsite support staff from Xtime and Dealertrack I needed someone at the dealership to take the reins and be the cheerleader for the store."

Over the last 10 – 15 years the skills required for service advisors has dramatically changed. It is still important to possess some knowledge of vehicle systems; however, we are looking for Apple-store type people to document our customer's needs and provide a positive service experience."

### Dealing with Holdouts

Nonetheless, holdouts to technology changes and upgrades, and to other manifestations of cultural transformation, remain a challenge for many dealers. So let's revisit and drill more deeply into this issue that we first addressed in the last chapter and see how the leadership of some customer-centric dealerships handle it.

---

*"You've got to build rapport with the customer before you have the right to ask for the sale. So, I stand true to that [in fixed operations] and expect our advisors to build rapport with the customer and do the walk-around, before we have the right to ask for the sale or to ask for the menu items."*

---

Sometimes it's service advisors who simply don't want to use tablets or iPads or take a more holistic approach to getting the customer engaged in the service visit.

Newsome, for instance, says that she's lost advisors at Vaden over the last several years simply because they don't want to change how they process the customer.

"A lot of them were our veteran advisors who learned how to write service with a clipboard and a write-up sheet," she says. "So, they weren't necessarily focused on the walk-around, or on building rapport, on chatting with the customer. They're really wanting to get the car back to the shop, take a look at it, and then approach the customer to make a sale then.

"I started on the variable side of the business, and it was drilled into my head that you've got to build rapport with the customer before you have the right to ask for the sale. So, I stand true to that [in fixed operations] and expect our advisors to build rapport with the customer and do the walk-around, before we have the right to ask for the sale or to ask for the menu items."

And at some dealerships, it's the technicians who don't want to embrace change, often about using MPI software.

At Hilton Head Honda, Muth says, "The technicians are probably the hardest group to motivate in terms of using [MPI software] all the time. But I think they understand it as well. It's their money, and when they recommend work, if they can use the software and track it, it goes back to them if the customer declines it.

"It's just something I have to keep reminding them to do. And I do a monthly report where I can track who was using it and who was not using it, how many hours they're recommending, how many hours are being sold, and so forth."

Fowler Auto Group has been able to boost its inspection rate to 88 percent of all ROs, with closing rates rising to 18 percent and sales from inspections of nearly $600,000, by just hammering away at implementation by its staff.

"The service managers need to be constantly communicating with the front, service advisors, and the back, technicians," says Pelkey, director of service operations for Fowler. "If one of the techs isn't going to use it, we need to go back and talk with them. Explain the benefits to them. We may have to do this multiple times and show them shortcuts."

Sweeney of Fletcher-Jones agrees. "We work through all of those obstacles, but you're going to have your negative people who, no matter what you do, are going to find a problem with it," he tells me. "You just keep knocking those objections out of the way, taking them away until they've got no more objections and they've got a tool where they have to say, 'OK, I guess there's value.'"

As a result, Fletcher Jones now does inspections on 99.5 percent of the cars that come through the shop, and its closing rates of up-sold services on those cars runs between 35 percent and 40 percent.

"They can see the value of doing all of these things from the write-up process to the inspection process to emailing the inspection to the approval," Sweeney says.

If internal resistance remains formidable, enlightened management just needs to be persistent and work with the hold-outs by showing how well the software and the multi-point inspection process perform over time.

## Reinforcing the Customer-Technology Connection

At an Ohio multi-point dealership chain, resistance reared its ugly head in a variety of ways. One big front in the battle was over multi-point inspections and software and how well—or poorly—employees were faring in creating ASRs and converting extra service opportunities into service sales.

"Now, this is difficult for people who don't have a level of maturity where they can have a real-world human discussion about things—people who are afraid the minute their work is scrutinized that someone is going to fire them or be mean to them," says the fixed-operations director of the company.

"But you can't reassure people like that enough that this is a training tool. That we're a football team and, you know what a football team does on Monday morning after the game is over? They look at the tapes.

"Our Monday [performance management] calls are the equivalent to a football team watching tapes from the last game.

"How did we do last week? Where did we leave opportunity on the table last week? There's not a football team on the planet that comes in on Monday afternoon, watches film and goes, 'Wow, that was a perfect game!' You know, and they don't fire the whole team because of one imperfect game.

"They go, 'OK, here are about a dozen things we can work on to beat that.' That's what we're doing."

The service executive continues, "We have never once said to a service advisor, 'You need to start selling more work. Your closing ratio stinks.' If we have an advisor that can't close work, the software will make that apparent over time. And the way to address that is that over an extended period of time you analyze the pattern, if it's a serious enough problem that we're really leaving business on the table.

"If the advisor is following what we asked them to do, and printing a booklet with every RO, our assumption is if you're going to the trouble of printing a booklet, you're going over it with the customer. And you've done your job.

"Some weeks everybody's going to buy something; some weeks, they are not. But the good news is all that information stacks in the system, and when the customer is back in six or nine months, the first thing that's going to pop up in the tool and you're going to get a second crack at it. We are fine with all of that.

---

*"Our Monday [performance management] calls are the equivalent to a football team watching tapes from the last game."*

---

"The non-negotiable for us is that you will do multi-point inspections. As an advisor you will print booklets and you will text your ASRs. As a technician, you will do a multi-point inspection on every car. Those are effort things. If you're giving effort, you are going to get results using this software."

At the same time, problematic advisors and technicians find other ways to drag their feet. "We had one advisor who decided he was going to do whatever he wanted to do, like he has for most of the last several years," the Ohio fixed-operations guy recounts with a chuckle. "And he's gotten away with it at some level because we've never had a really good, objective, quantifiable evaluation tool.

"So, one of his early plays in our Monday meetings about the new scheduling platform was that his customers don't have cell phones. His customers—for a luxury brand—'don't have cell phones.' He said they were older guys, they don't text, they don't do this, they don't do that.

"But over the next few weeks, as other writers would fill in and write ROs for his customers, it became readily apparent that somehow for those other writers, these customers had cell phones. And not only that, they were responding affirmatively to ASR requests.

"And we were selling work via text, and we were even processing payment via text. So miraculously, all of a sudden, after four or five sessions, his customers started figuring out how to use cell phones."

Scott, the service head for Bob Johnson Chevrolet, developed one way to counter this kind of foot-dragging.

"Letting the software review the data in weekly performance calls is the most effective way to make sure the program is implemented," he tells me. "It's difficult for people to argue against national averages and things like that.

"The typical excuses you get for people not doing things—'It's different here'; 'Our customers are different'; blah, blah, blah—you can defuse a lot of that stuff early in the process by talking about the fact that the software covers literally thousands of customers and has huge piles of aggregated data for whatever brand you're talking about.

"And when you have a number of advisors and a number of technicians, the performance against the averages puts a little bit of accountability into it where if people aren't following processes or are under-performing, or they need training, being able to go through that on a weekly basis is super-important."

## Tying Incentives to Technology Adoption

At the same time, compensation of your people should be tied as closely as possible to running a customer-centric dealership. Instead of incentives that only reflect transactions, pay plans should at least be partly reflective of customer-retention levels that are measured by criteria that reflect the dealership's loyalty objectives.

Monteverde, at Ferman Chevrolet-Volvo, found that this motivational method has worked well for overcoming internal resistance at his shops.

"We keep piling more and more on our technicians and more on our service staff," he says. "And so, they want to see an immediate benefit, or you start losing control. You can pound your fist and you can throw some money at it, some bonuses, but it's got to be a good product. It's got to work as designed, or people get discouraged. And for the most part it has worked.

"About 70 percent of advisors bought in right away, and the 30 percent who didn't were mostly part of the older generation. They like new technology, but they like to see what it's going to do. So, for those folks, we made it fun, such as contests for how many ASRs were sold.

"Now we have a contest every month in whatever we're falling behind on, and we make it fun in terms of money. But everybody started to click in the same direction within six months.

"Such as this month, it's $100 a man for usage over 70%. Most of my guys are in teams. I want to pay them the money and keep them supercharged on it. And it's all or nothing. So, what you find is that the guys who are a little weak get some help from some of the younger techy guys who say, 'Hey, man, I'll help you with that. We want to win. We want an extra $100.'

"We also have contest for CSI. My techs have always been paid up to $150 a month extra for their score on 'Fix It Right the First Time.' And advisors are paid up to $300 a month on overall service satisfaction. We pay out to keep it fun—you know, $2 each tire you sell, or $2 for an alignment, whatever."

Temecula Hyundai played a bit of hardball with balky service writers.

"The service writers were saying that they were very frustrated and were just going to give up on the software," Nicholson recalls. "They said it was taking too much time. And I said, 'You're right, you're right—we've tried it for three days and it's just not working out for you. No problem. Don't use the tablets.

"'But know this: You're only going to get paid your commission on the repair orders that have an MPI done through the tablet. So, here's the good news: You get to decide what ROs you get paid on, and which ones you don't.'

"That solved the problem. With me, they had to know that discipline has teeth in it. And I did it in such a way that I made it 'their idea,' because of course they want to get paid.

"I had someone on my quick-lube rack who just dug in his heels and said, 'I'm just not going to do it.' So I said, 'OK, I get it. But can I let you in on a little secret?' And he says, 'Yeah.' And I say, 'Well, you're not going to do it somewhere else. Because you're not going to not do it with me.' I got back from lunch and his toolbox was gone and the rest was history.

"You're going to have that. I want to save all of the service writers and technicians, but I can't. And the fact that I've lost only one—I'm good with that. It's really for the betterment of the team."

## Customer-Centric Change is Your Responsibility

As all these examples illustrate, forging a new culture comes down to leadership, and that includes dealing smartly and decisively with holdouts. Unfortunately, hold-outs are often still enabled by inexperienced managers who can't or won't stand up to employees who impede progress.

I've been working with dealers for more than 30 years, and it's always been, "Bob's been here a long time and the customers love him, and he won't use the tablets. And because he won't use it, other advisors won't use it. So, we're going to remove them."

But recently I'm seeing less tolerance for resistance to change, expressed in ways such as, "You know what—there's an utter need for this system." It's not so much an age thing but an ability-to-adapt thing. And savvy service managers are getting the adaptation they need, one way or another.

Or, as Jim Coleman puts it, "Tech is just not that hard anymore. I don't think it's overtaxing anyone. So, if someone isn't using it, you need to find that right person who will. It doesn't matter if you think they're your best guy; in reality they're not your best guy. He gets the biggest gross for you because he pushes customers but in the process he circumvents everything and aggravates employees and customers alike."

And in the end, treating people right, giving them every opportunity to sign on to participating in a customer-centric enterprise, usually carries the day.

"The biggest hurdle we have today is that technicians aren't just bodies," says Monteverde of Ferman Chevrolet-Volvo. "They are people who want to work and make a career. Not so many years ago, some of them were working at a burger shop and thought the grass would be greener at an automotive dealership.

"So, promote from within and keep quality people around you. That takes a lot of time, and nurturing, and coaching, and mentoring. And it's no different than what somebody did for me years ago. I try to do the same thing for the folks that are here."

## "You have to give everyone the 'why'.

Great dealership cultures also emphasize that a winning customer experience is tied intrinsically to everyone in the service department—not just service advisors. Sure, the front-line folks have to get things started on the right foot with customers. But technicians also have a key role in providing a great dealership experience.

Darrel Ferguson makes the point well: "By far, the biggest challenge is culture, changing people's mindset and long-term behavior.

You have to give everyone the 'why'. Employees are often just told to do something—that's a very militant style.

"The problem is, if they don't understand the 'why' they just go through the motions. For example, getting the technicians to do consistent multi-point inspections. Showing the technician what is ultimately presented to the customer helps them to visualize that part and understand their importance in the whole process."

## Key Takeaways:

- Your culture will be the most important determinant of the success of your efforts to become customer-centric.
- Leadership from the top is the biggest factor in establishing the right culture.
- Expect resistance as your people adjust to new expectations and new ways of interacting with one another and with customers.
- Pay plans are one of the best ways to encourage compliance with, and promotion of, a customer-centric culture.
- Whether you succeed in establishing a new culture comes down to good—or poor —management and persistence.

There are great lessons here about leadership setting the example, and also importantly that no matter your organization, small or large, you can create or improve a customer-centric culture. But you need to get started.

And then you must make sure those cultural imperatives are reflected in how you hire, promote and cull people at your dealership. That's what we're going to discuss next.

# Chapter 11

Hiring Customer-Centric Talent and Teams

If you aspire to a world-class customer-centric culture, maybe the most significant change you could make is to look for something different in the people you hire.

In this time of tight labor, during which dealers are having to leave no stone unturned to find and keep good people throughout their service operation, it can be difficult to elevate your expectations when you feel like you're bending over backwards just to make a hire.

But if you truly want to move toward a customer-centric dealership, hiring is the last place you want to settle.

Look at our illustration: People are one of the essential components of that crucial Outer Circle of elements.

Let's start with perhaps the most important area of hiring for any dealer wanting a customer-centric enterprise: service advisors.

While doing dealer interviews for *Fast Lane*, it became clear that the top quality sought in a service advisor these days is no longer technical acumen.

In a word, it's empathy—the ability to understand where the customer is coming from in a particular moment, on a particular day, and in general, and to tailor a satisfying, customer-focused experience around these perceptions.

Though advisors are pretty much the face of the dealership to the general public once they buy their car, for decades the general process for hiring service advisors was simply this: "That tech is really good at what he does. We should promote him to service advisor."

Of course, the problem with that approach was taking someone who was a productive tech and sticking them in front of the public without any training—and often, in gross contradiction to what his personality and their intellectual and social fits would suggest—because they knew the product really well.

"As technology changes, we're finding that sometimes the best service advisors aren't the same people you would have targeted 10 to 15 years ago," says the leader of the large midwestern dealer group. "We're looking for Apple-store type people to wait on our guests and make that experience better, not a technician who didn't want to turn wrenches anymore."

In fact, it's becoming more and more apparent to service managers that what they need in advisors is no longer the product-knowledge gurus, but someone who's empathetic.

---

*"We're looking for Apple-store type people to wait on our guests and make that experience better."*

---

## Find Your Talent-Feeders

Besides the Starbucks barista and Apple-store "genius," another model that some dealers envision for their hiring objective these days is someone who's good enough to work at a theme park, interacting with customers. For Temecula Hyundai, in the heart of Southern California, hiring these people can actually be a reality.

"For customer-facing roles, I want to hire people who have come from other customer-facing roles, from Disneyland, SeaWorld, McDonald's—whatever the case may be—but not people who are inward-facing or technical," Nicholson says. "I don't need service advisors who can fix a car but fix a customer. Techs just can't do that—some can, but they are rare.

"So, I look for people who come from places that set the bar high for customer service. Once I get that person, things can change in a couple of days."

---

*"I don't need service advisors who can fix a car but fix a customer."*

---

For service advisors, Williams formerly of Del Grande Dealer Group follows the empathy trail and looks "for people who have customer-facing experience [whom] we can train," such as waiters.

"They know how to deal with conflict: 'This food is too cold,'" he says. "And they might take some time to understand how our business model works, but we don't have to teach them the skills to make customers happy because, living off tips, they already believe in service. They also know how to handle conflict and sell stuff."

Turske says that Fox Motors has changed its approach significantly because of the empathy factor and other requirements of the new era.

"Even though in most cases prior experience is required when hiring employees, we need to identify potential employees that display the ability to adapt and change with technology. We are looking for someone who can be progressive and have problem solving traits."

"It's not only about how long someone has been a service advisor or how much monthly parts and labor sales they generate. We need somebody that can adapt to our rapidly changing environment."

"In the past typical interview questions could be, "Tell me what DMS you've used.' Now, it's "Tell me about a time when you had to change a habit that you've been doing for a long time."

"We find that most of the new advisors that are coming into our business have little trouble adapting to updated check-in process because they don't have to unlearn years of habits."

"Unfortunately, we did lose a small number of employees along the way that did not want to adapt to our service drive technology and inspection process. We did consider this when making the decision to change but felt like the long-term benefits were worth the short-term disruption."

Manson, the former service-operations executive, says that in recruiting customer-facing employees for dealerships he would "look for someone who wasn't afraid to have a conversation, whether that was a positive one or a negative one."

He also probed for "integrity. I would ask [interviewees] to talk about their past and tell me about an experience where you felt uncomfortable, or where someone was doing something improper. What did you do?"

When someone wanted a job with one of Manson's dealerships, he would investigate their organizational skills, if possible, with one simple exercise: He would walk the person back out to their car and peek into it.

"That told me a lot, because how they kept their personal life in order would be how they would keep their professional life," Manson says.

Motorcars Group goes so far as to avoid hiring as service advisors people who've worked as service advisors in other dealerships.

"We've just found that they're not going to make it long-term for us," Gile says. "We have to grow them from the ground up—that's where we've had our best success."

If they hire experienced service advisors, he tells me, they tend to come from express chains such as Jiffy Lube. "They're used to using a more personal touch, and they don't work at the slower speed of a traditional dealership," Gile says. "We can develop them more quickly than someone from another Honda dealership."

## Create Your Own Proving Ground

New service advisors at Motorcars may start on the express-service line, for instance, and graduate to the regular service department.

The biggest pipeline for new advisors, believe it or not, is Motorcars valets: About a half-dozen of them each year move up into advisor roles or into parts positions.

"Valets are kind of the pipeline for the dealership as a whole, because they're able to understand our culture," he says. "They're actually the face of the dealership, constantly creating that customer experience. If you've been to Disney, one of the most important positions they have at their parks is the people who pick up the trash, because they're the ones who interact the most with customers."

Another way Motorcars finds employee diamonds in the rough is by considering people "who aren't lighting it up" on the showroom floor but have a great touch with customers. Instead of moving them out of the dealership altogether, they'll move them into a greeter positions in the service department.

"They can create a better guest experience," Gile says. "They're not necessarily the most expensive employee. They didn't excel in one position, but they have great empathy and can move up in another."

> *"If you've been to Disney, one of the most important positions they have at their parks is the people who pick up the trash, because they're the ones who interact the most with customers."*

Nicholson at Temecula Hyundai is finding the same thing, as the dealership transfers middling salespeople into effective service advisors.

The dealership now employs two quick-lube writers "who were young salespeople who were incredible with customers on the sales floor, in their twenties," he says. "But [the showroom] was going to let them go because they just couldn't hit the store minimum of selling eight cars a month."

Why look twice at two young people who couldn't sell enough cars to stick on the variable side?

"These two were young and in a sales environment with a lot of old crusties, older salespeople who've got an established client base," Nicholson explains. "It's a tough gig, and to some degree you've got to be aggressive when you're in the showroom.

"But I saw talent. And if they've got talent and they're teachable, we wanted them. They've worked out great."

## Building Your Technician Talent Pool

Of course, hiring the right service advisors is only part of the equation. If you don't have people to fix the automobiles, it doesn't matter how good a dealership's digital marketing is or how much empathy you hire for the service lane.

The best service managers have been getting creative in their efforts to recruit and retain capable technicians.

Some dealers are getting help in this regard from OEMs. Audi and Jaguar Land Rover, among others, have launched massive—and effective—programs over the last few years to recruit military veterans for the service departments of their dealers.

In addition to the technical expertise that military vets can bring to an auto service department, many managers like their characteristic discipline, maturity, focus on quality and attention to detail.

In addition to the technical expertise that military vets can bring to an auto service department, many managers like their characteristic discipline, maturity, focus on quality and attention to detail.

On the dealership side, Fox Motors, unsurprisingly, is one of the groups that is robustly attacking the challenge of finding and keeping good technicians. Jack Turske tells me:

"Approximately three years ago we initiated a technician mentoring program where we team up someone that would like to be a technician with a mentor. As part of the program they receive a set of tools with a value of almost $4,000. After successful completion of the program the tools become theirs."

Del Grande Dealer Group sends managers into community-college auto-repair programs to recruit advisors and technicians. A couple of times a year, Williams and others trek to each of four community colleges in the market and search for interns.

"The first time, I go in and tell them about the industry and how much money they can make, and the second time I go in and buy them lunch and ask if they want to be interns and tell them our philosophy and about the job and how important it is to do it correctly.

"No one else is in front of these classes, and I get the cream of the crop," Williams tells me.

Del Grande has great success with this effort: It has brought in 14 to 18 service interns each year for the last five years, and about 60 percent of them have stuck. "That's a good ratio," Williams says.

Such stories underscore one of the most important realities of creating a customer-centric dealership: You must build it on the right people.

## Key Takeaways:

- Hiring the right people is critical to transform your culture, and to create a customer-centric operation.
- Bring on board and promote the right service advisors by seeking today's most important quality in interacting with customers: empathy.
- Get creative in searching for new-era advisors, including focusing on other service industries.
- Don't forget to do an internal search for non-traditional candidates.
- Searching for technicians in a labor-tight environment requires thinking outside of the (tool) box.

Feel like you're well on your way toward understanding what it takes to establish a customer-centric dealership?

Good—remain focused. Because, next, we're going to discuss some of the distractions that can take your eye off the ball.

# Chapter 12

Stop Chasing "Squirrels"

As we've explained, becoming truly customer-centric starts with leaders and their philosophy of how to run the business, and will then spread to management and through managers to the rest of the organization.

You will certainly have to provide training, and customer-centric approaches must imbue your hiring practices. You may also have to upgrade some people who can't or aren't willing to make the transition. Improve your culture.

With People and Training, you transform your Processes, and the underlying Technologies that support your processes.

But there will be speed bumps. And what I like to call "squirrels" you'll have to chase.

In fact, while you're in the process of making your break to a customer-centric operating philosophy, which is difficult in and of itself, many dealers and service managers are also pressed on every side.

President Dwight Eisenhower said, "I have two kinds of problems, the urgent and the important. The urgent are not important, and the important are never urgent."

I think this wisdom can be applied to service-department leaders. You are handed lots of distractions that everyone else thinks may be important, but which top management must minimize so that you can keep your eyes on the goal posts.

Service managers get pulled in a lot of tactical directions, being yanked at by their techs, service advisors, managers from other departments, the dealer—and, of course, customers.

In addition to the day-to-day of dealing with heat customers and reluctant employees, service managers can get distracted by illness, vacations and turnover.

At a recent industry advisory session, I spent time with Christopher Ouellette, the vice president of operations for Long Lewis Auto Group, a six-store operation, including the oldest and largest Ford dealer in Alabama and the winner of more Presidents' Awards for customer satisfaction than any other dealer in the country.

He told me that, in the past, some of his service leaders were "so accustomed to fixing angry customers that they thought that was the norm, they didn't feel they were adding value for the dealership unless they were busy putting out fires. We had customers that were upset, techs were upset, and they figured that was normal. They were used to being reactive when they needed to be proactive" He adds "today, our managers are pivoting to a more proactive, technology driven mindset of management."

Unfortunately, this certainly fits with the previous perception of the service manager: someone who adds value by being reactive and keeps the heat away from the dealer and/or general manager.

Also, service managers can get distracted by initiatives from the factory that demand their attention, ranging from goodwill issues to reacting to J.D. Power scores.

And dealership owners can distract their service leaders when they unleash a bunch of really big squirrels that, of course, their management charges feel compelled to chase.

These can be various day-to-day distractions or what I call the 20 Group Watusi: A dealer comes back from a 20 Group meeting with his pants on fire with "new" ideas for the service department that they want implemented "immediately."

What's interesting about these types of distractions is they usually fall into two buckets: The dealer has an idea for how to optimize ROs ("Let's be more transaction-centric," which is the wrong direction) or something that is very specific to being customer-centric.

The problem with this is if you don't have the fundamental elements in place of both your Inner Circle and Outer Circle for a customer-centric dealership, then trying to implement highly tactical elements of a customer-centric strategy will probably fail.

Hence, even a dealer who's pivoted toward establishing a customer-centric enterprise can inadvertently handcuff his or her service managers by tethering them to micro priorities that get in the way of achieving larger goals.

Of course, the best way for service managers and dealers to ensure they're not chasing squirrels that get in the way of the goal is to forge a partnership between the owner or general manager, and the service leader.

Make sure fixed operations not only have the budget and proper staffing levels to help achieve a truly customer-centric service department but also that they share in the philosophy and strategy behind the pivot.

### Key Takeaways:

- Distractions can slow or stop the overhaul of your culture and your focusing on improving the customer experience.
- Minimize "chasing squirrels" get in the way of your objectives.

# Chapter 13

## Making Your Marketing Customer-Centric

What good is it to establish a customer-centric operation if you aren't telling people about it effectively?

Let's flash back to that service scheduling stat—nearly half of customers who could have used a self-directed scheduling tool didn't because they didn't know they could.

Dealers have a similar problem in variable operations when they adopt more transparent pricing and sales processes. Unless they're telling the world about their new way of doing business, customers won't know, and they'll be just as defensive as ever.

Effective marketing for retention of existing customers, as well as for new prospects, is a crucial component of that inner circle of characteristics that makes for an enduring dealership that grows profitably.

Dealers who are pioneering in this area are relying on e-mail campaigns and other digital channels, are incorporating pricing transparency as part of their marketing strategy.

There's still some need for media advertising by car dealers for their sales operations in newspapers, TV and radio ads, but targeted digital marketing to both prospects and existing customers is reducing that role all the time.

There have been incredible shifts in the ways advertising dollars are spent by dealers, away from traditional media and toward internet/ digital spending.

You can see this shift by comparing the advertising allocations from 2014 to 2017. Internet spend has increased from 26.3 percent to 55.4 percent, while direct mail has dropped from 10.7 percent to 7.2 percent.

But don't believe that direct mail is "dead" this still represents dealers spending more than $900 million on direct mail in 2017:

Digital marketing is taking over and creating new outreach opportunities for dealers' service operations because it's highly targeted and therefore more cost-effective.

Service has never have been heavily advertised in media, and traditionally service marketing has been done by using direct mail for service reminders or service prospect coupon sheets.

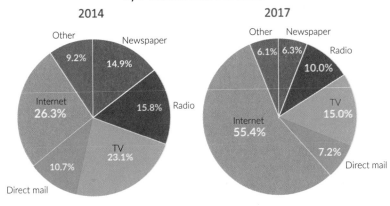

## Advertising Expenditures
### by Medium 2014 & 2017

**2014**

- Other 9.2%
- Newspaper 14.9%
- Radio 15.8%
- TV 23.1%
- Direct mail 10.7%
- Internet 26.3%

**2017**

- Other 6.1%
- Newspaper 6.3%
- Radio 10.0%
- TV 15.0%
- Direct mail 7.2%
- Internet 55.4%

Source: NADA

But now, new marketing methods and digital tools are enabling service managers to leverage minimal marketing resources for big gains in customer retention and expansion of crucial lifetime relationships.

One of the drivers for this change for customer-centric dealers is that they want to focus as many of their marketing resources as possible on customer retention, on creating stickiness that will ensure they're building customer relationships for life.

Another contributor to this trend is the availability of very effective digital marketing programs that can be precisely targeted and timed based on the need and status of each individual customer and vehicle.

You can customize the messaging and cadence and fulfill using multi-channel communications to retain loyal customers, capture prospects or new customers, and re-capture defected customers, sometimes known as "lost souls."

This sophisticated software now manages customer relationships, as well as other digital programs and channels, and gives service managers unprecedented marketing capabilities—and ones that are individually targeted to an extent that hasn't been possible in the service business.

In fact, given these robust new marketing methods -- and most consumers' expectations for customized approaches by brands these days -- dealership service marketing can be effectively personalized to each vehicle and its owner.

But each message must inform them of something that has context and relevance to that customer and their vehicle.

Marketing in this way also can establish a virtual cycle where digital communications not only help bring people in the door but also get customers more and more invested in using the dealership's technology platform. In turn, that leaves them more inclined to answer the dealership's marketing calls to action.

It's been a bumpy road for service departments to get to the point where they've been able to use digital marketing effectively, and in the highly integrated way that customers require these days from the brands that win their business.

But now there's no excuse for a dealership service department not to have a highly relevant digital-marketing platform that advances the customer-centric experience in significant ways.

## Focus on Retention

To reach both prospects and customers, to get them into—or back into—the dealership and have an opportunity to work on a lifetime relationship with them, a dealer's marketing must be clear and concise, have an easily understood call to action, and include a way to fulfill it.

Del Grande Dealer Group used to have an ad hoc approach to marketing their service departments, but recently the company consolidated its marketing under a universal image.

"We want our advertising to be branded Del Grande Dealer Group and be store specific. And we have to make sure it's marketing that customers will go for and that if there's an offer, it's easy for them to click on and use."

Indeed, your marketing can't put out dead-end offers. It's got to be personalized and multichannel, available on a smartphone, desktop computer or tablet. You've got to meet the customer where they want to be, and the call to action has got to be integrated into a larger, holistic, technology-enhanced experience. (That last point is especially important because dealers historically have been challenged about this.)

Yet even in an era in which digital marketing offers many possibilities, be wary of the fact that it isn't all the same, and it isn't all equally effective. The best and by far the most cost-effective methods are those that focus on customer retention, not casting around for new customers.

For example, some dealers have tried search-based marketing in service but have found it lacking. "So many people seem to be investing in SEO, but I'm not seeing that it's useful for generating transactions," says Ruprecht, fixed-operations director at Koons. "Our experience is that it seems to be somewhat useful for brand building.

---

*"I'd rather spend $2,000 retaining my own customers than go out and spend $2,000 to find maybe some new customers in my PMA."*

---

"We've seen a couple of our stores schedule one appointment out of the whole month of an SEO campaign, or two appointments for the whole month," he says. "So, I spent $2,000 or $3,000 and it wasn't worth it."

"My car is my safety and my family's safety," he says. "I'm not going to just go for the cheap. Some people would. I understand that. But if people want to go to a dealership, most of them are going to look for dealerships around where they live. And I'd rather spend $2,000 retaining my own customers than go out and spend $2,000 to find maybe some new customers in my PMA."

Instead, Koons finds that its monthly e-mail blast to customers helps educate them about the benefits of online scheduling, which drives response in ever-increasing rates of adoption by service customers as they read, accept and internalize the messaging in the marketing e-mail.

Therefore, Ruprecht favors e-mail marketing, in large part because it targets existing customers for more business rather than invest dollars hoping to nab a handful of new customers.

"The best and cheapest way of reaching service customers is e-mail campaigns on a weekly basis," Ruprecht says. "We target our database at each store. We say, OK, we have customers that we haven't seen for four months to 12 months. We need to contact them, just to say, 'Hey, we haven't seen you. Here are our specials'—basically, whatever we have on our website, we send to our customers.

"They don't have go to www.koonsofsilverspring.com to see what our service specials are; they're right there in the email. 'We'd like to see you in our service lane' in such and such a period of time. And, 'To schedule an appointment, click here.' And that takes them to the online scheduler.

"So, we've designed it to be as simple as possible for the customer—we're only a couple clicks away, so the call to action is very easy to complete."

Ramzy Handal of Jim Koons Automotive Group shares a similar view for search-engine advertising. "People say you have to spend a lot of money on SEM and social media, but if it doesn't equal a customer in my service lane, then it's a load of crap.

"I assign our marketing campaigns an ID number, and we track it through our BDC and match it against our traffic report and look at the end result. Those SEM-type campaigns don't have much impact on traffic."

## Elements of E-mail Marketing Success

Indeed, most dealership service departments that are finding success with digital marketing are relying heavily on e-mail modules that integrate with their scheduling, engagement and inspection software.

As much as he dismisses search-engine-based campaigns, Handal of Jim Koons Automotive heartily endorses e-mail-based marketing.

"E-mail campaigns sent weekly are by far the best and cheapest" advertising, he says. "We target our existing customers; we send our specials; and we tell them, 'We'd like to see you.' We include a service-appointment link.

Muth, of Hilton Head Honda, echoes Handal. "We're in a small, community that's growing pretty rapidly, so you kind of half expect growth in ROs with the growth of the area," he says. "But I also feel like it has a lot to do with our marketing software as well.

"With keeping customers in the loop on marketing, and then the service lifecycle, from start to finish—I believe that helps," he explains. "With our e-mail marketing we have the thank-you e-mail that goes out after service, and if there's ever an issue, people will reply to that e-mail and I'll be able to resolve any issue they may have—or at least have the opportunity to resolve it."

Muth says that his predecessor at Hilton Head Honda "didn't have an in-house marketing campaign—something that tapped into our database of customers and our DMS. Nothing was in place that marketed toward these customers; it was all advertising either through Honda or through local outlets."

But then he began harnessing the service department's new software platform. Hilton Head Honda began sending promotional specials that played to price sensitivity for specific services.

"It allowed us to market to our own clientele using our own coupons and so forth," Muth says. "And that has helped tremendously because I can see the effect almost instantaneously.

"I can say, 'Hey, Thursday is looking light. I'm going to send out this coupon on Wednesday,' and you'll see the phones light up. It's insane that you can see the instant gratification. And that has helped retention just by keeping people in the loop and keeping active e-mails with them, reminding them that we're here and that we've got a special going on."

Fletcher Jones uses e-mail to reach out to customers with recalls, using a recall-data provider. "Manufacturers know who most people in your market are, but they won't share that information with you for legal reasons," says Sweeney.

"So, there are services that can only reach out to recall customers. They have the ability to get data that's not available to normal marketing platforms. And there's no offer attached to it, which also gives you the ability to text to customers and say, 'Hey, you have a safety recall.' The response rate is off the charts.

Fletcher Jones also is among the many dealers who are using e-mailings and promotional deals to pursue lost customers with a combination of digital follow-up and price elasticity.

"We said why don't we find a way to sell cost-maintenance packages offline?" Sweeney recalls. "We're starting with our lost customers. 'We've got you; we just haven't seen you in 18 months.'

"Now we have the ability to e-mail that package out. These are customers who currently don't do business with us, or we haven't seen them in over 18 months. Each customer we send to also will get a second e-mail, and then the third e-mail will be an offer that they can't bypass—like two 'A' services for the price of one."

Sweeney tells me, "I don't really care because I don't have them anyway, so what do I care if they're buying something at below cost, if it puts them in our service drive? The ability to put someone in the drive at any cost is—well, we've just got to do it."

"That's going to evolve into what I call 'hot deals,' where customers can buy a front-end alignment for half the price for just a one-hour period online and fulfill it later. You buy it online for, say, $59.95. All these are conquests and lost customers.

## Tying in Time-Sensitive Offers

Sweeney says one effective tactic is to send e-mails to target consumers at the most optimal times and then only give them a short window to act on the deal.

"It could be an hour, it could be two hours, it could be three hours, because we know there are windows and peak times where people look at their e-mail," he explains. "So, we'll base it off those peak times, such as between 11 a.m. and 1 p.m.

"We work with our loyal customers and give them good offers, they're coming eventually anyway. We don't have to be too aggressive. On the other hand, it's a loss with service conquests. Give away whatever it takes to pull them in your service drive.

"A lot of dealers are still doing it with direct mail. There's still some value in that. But they keep on hammering their loyal customers over and over again, and there's no focus on the lost and conquest customers. Even big marketing companies don't do a good job with those customers."

Sweeney has concluded, "With technology, I think we can give them a real offer that's tangible and they see value in it—and to motivate them to respond to a call to action.

"There's got to be something motivating about it. What we're working on right now is the subject line: 'Do you want to save money?' or whatever it is. What's going to make them click it open. We'll watch click-throughs. We'll try different things to keep it fresh and relevant, and at some point it will resonate with you."

I believe that dealers should practice more of this kind of promotional aggressiveness with digital methods. In conjunction with practicing promotional aggressiveness, I believe that dealerships should practice price transparency and advertise their service prices.

Remember that in today's world, it's, "Advantage consumer." It's one where pricing information is more transparent than ever in many other commercial transactions. And where price transparency — whether you're buying a big-screen TV or getting your oil changed—is expected. Remember the three fundamentals of online selling: tell me what I need, when I can get it and what it costs.

Consumers are already very accustomed to this with car sales. Consumers can go online and get a fairly good idea of the cost of that vehicle—a historically unprecedented level of transparency that's been available for years. It's dramatically changed the way dealers merchandise and price new vehicles.

Dealership service departments, too, can leverage price transparency both from the very practical aspect of bringing customers in during light times on the schedule, and as a way of building a customer-centric enterprise by making customers understand that your service department is genuinely trying to satisfy them and to keep their business.

### Publish Prices or Perish

All of this takes us to my ultimate point: You must publish your service prices, especially for your most commonly requested services.

When I speak to dealership audiences, roughly half the members state that they currently publish prices. To demonstrate the point, we go through an exercise. I start by asking the crowd, "How many of you flew here today?" Most hands go up. "How many bought your ticket online?" Most of the same hands go up.

"OK, how many of you bought a ticket from the airline that said, 'I have the flight that you want, and I'll tell you what the ticket costs when you get to the airport?'"

Of course, it's good for a laugh, but then the point sinks in: Isn't that the same thing that your dealership is doing, basically, if you offer service appointments but don't publish your prices?

*Remember the three fundamentals of online selling: tell me what I need, when I can get it and what it costs.*

Now I'm not naïve—I know why you're not publishing your prices. It's fear of the unknown: You're afraid that you're too expensive compared to the competition, you'll get price-shopped and you'll lose the business.

That's why dealers should be performing competitive price analyses in your local market area, at least twice per year,—and then adjust your prices accordingly.

Let me be perfectly clear: I am *not* advocating that you need to be the lowest-priced provider. But you do need to be transparent and offer a fair and reasonable price.

Then you will be armed with knowledge and can act with confidence. Then publish those prices on your website, in your menus, in your scheduling system, in your service marketing. Hang the price comparison in your service lane! It's a big move in the direction of being customer-centric.

It also might yield more benefits than you think. Cox research shows consumers generally believe that service at car dealerships is more expensive than at the local Midas or Pep Boys, and certainly more expensive than at an independent shop.

And yet the same research shows that even for a commodity service such as an oil change, dealers typically are priced at or near what the other guys are asking.

## Are Dealers Pricing Services Fairly?
### What are consumers paying? Oil Change Snapshot

Source: Cox Automotive 2018 Service Industry Study

As vehicles get more complex, consumers associate product expertise with the seller—the dealer. You also have factory-certified technicians, OE-approved and sophisticated diagnostic equipment, genuine factory parts and a great facility.

We should be marketing the hell out of our product expertise, technology-enhanced experience and fair and reasonable pricing.

Again: Advantage, dealers.

## The Power of Price-Matching and Perks

Still dubious? What do you think of when you consider Progressive Insurance? You pretty much think that their prices are the lowest and that they've got some funny advertising with Flo.

But did you realize that when Progressive invites an online price comparison by consumers, sometimes their prices aren't the lowest? What they do is sell the value of what they offer: They're certainly less expensive than many competitors, plus they offer simplicity and convenience. The parallel here to dealers is powerful.

And there are other tactics you can use as well: If your prices aren't the lowest, you can always make it very clear to customers that you'll price-match.

Temecula Hyundai, for instance, has 80-percent retention on its PMA partly, Nicholson says, because the service department price-matches "anything that [customers] can get done at another dealership. I tell them: 'Bring it here.'

"And I don't even care if it's not another dealership. If it's a coupon from someone else, and they come in and say, 'They're offering me a front-end alignment for $39,' and they live in my PMA, I do the alignment for $39."

"And it gives me a chance to run their VIN through the recall system, and I will guarantee you that I can pick up a couple of hundred dollars just on open Hyundai recalls. It keeps them coming back.

"And it goes on. I've got another little card that I keep in my pocket. Part of our marketing when I came here was, 'We're making Temecula Hyundai great again.' We borrowed that slogan obviously. But a part of making Temecula Hyundai great again is to give the customer things they don't' get anywhere else that keep them coming back—in this instance a preferred $30 Visa gift card that's only good at my store.

"When a customer comes in and they've never been there before, or they come to get a recall done, they can use it toward anything they want: ice cream, t-shirts in my parts department, whatever. And there's no minimum purchase required to use the card.

"So, they can just come in here and drop $30 and it's on us. That's something normally you would only give someone who spends thousands of dollars in your store, right?

"Or we recommend something that's on the car based on our MPI. We say, 'Oh, by the way, we noticed that you've got one of our $30 preferred Visa cards. I can go ahead and apply that to this repair and take the price down from $199 to $169.' Rarely do they say no."

### Key Takeaways:

- Marketing for retention is one key to ensure long-term prosperity for your dealership.
- Harness digital marketing to both existing and potential customers.
- Be targeted and use price elasticity for promotions and specials that appeal to specific customers.
- Be price transparent and don't be afraid to publish your prices—sell the dealer advantages!

Creative and diligent use of e-mail marketing, price promotions and other tools can make a huge difference to your customers. That's why marketing for retention is an important part of the Inner Circle of elements that make for a customer-centric dealership.

Next, let's move back out to one of the important fundamental elements in our Outer Circle: your Facilities, and how to make them customer-centric.

# Chapter 14

Create Destination Dealerships

One of the best examples in the country of a customer-centric service operation is the Motorcars Honda dealership in Cleveland Heights, Ohio. With its facilities, it is emphasizing an important component of the Outer Circle that makes Motorcars one of the most customer-centric enterprises in the industry.

A 22-minute oil-change service is the key ingredient in the dealership's program for ultra-fast service.

In just two hours, 70 vehicles roll down the drive, and the dealership plans to provide the express service to 30,000 cars and trucks a year, with plans to double that capacity.

"We're getting business based on speed, transparency and price," says Trevor Gile.

Indeed, this moving assembly line for quick service has reduced customer wait times to under 30 minutes for an oil change, tire rotation, 20-point inspection and related services for a base price of $49.99. This creates a steady stream of vehicles into service bays for work that might otherwise have gone to aftermarket shops.

To get this nifty service, customers pull up to a huge garage door that leads to a 100-foot service drive with six stations. A valet carrying a tablet greets customers. The vehicle identification number discloses the maintenance and recall history of each car or truck, along with other information, according to *Automotive News.*

Customers can watch their vehicle being serviced on big TV monitors from padded seats behind a guardrail.

"The day of the customer not knowing what's being worked on with their car, and who's doing it, are fading away," Gile tells me. "We're eliminating the man behind the curtain. There's no place the car goes in our dealership where they can't see it.

"Before that, we had been presenting menus to the consumer using videos and pictures. But we wanted to take it to the next level where they could not only see pictures of what was being done to their cars but also look through a physical window. Every day we see more and more customers learning to walk and see their car getting worked on instead of sitting in the waiting area."

Motorcars also helps customers in other ways besides satisfying their curiosity; it helps them be more productive. The dealership built a high-end, high-speed car wash separate from the dealership facilities. Rainforest Car Wash is open to the public, but members of the Motorcars service loyalty program get a wash for free.

The Motorcars Honda dealership previously operated an in-bay car wash in the service area that ate up as much as $150,000 a year in costs for employees, electricity and water—and only provided what Gile calls "a sub-par wash."

"It was taking six to 15 minutes for people to get their cars washed, and it took a lot of employee time," he says. "It was such a bottleneck that it was hurting our CSI scores, because the perception was it was taking too long to get vehicles serviced.

"So, we built a giant tunnel wash on some of our used-car space, which provides a higher-level wash for customers," he explains. "It has given us an edge because the independents aren't doing this, and competitors in the dealership world aren't doing it. And we've turned the car wash from an expense to a really positive revenue stream.

"By moving the car wash off premises and giving customers a coupon for a wash, we have been able to cut the overall time down by several minutes," he says. "And the customers' perception is that the clock stops on our work when they leave, not as in the past until after we've washed the car. It's a separate transaction. It's been a huge thing for us."

In fact, Gile says, the car washes are Motorcars' second-most-profitable department. And their success has Motorcars "looking at other ways to bring things that we outsourced in the past, in-house, to produce a better experience for the customer, to increase revenue, or both."

Motorcars has been finding other ways to become more customer-centric even as it becomes financially fitter. For instance, the company began managing its loaner fleet much more closely. Employees were keeping them out too long for personal use and curbing that abuse has allowed Motorcars to save $90,000 a year because it could trim the size of its fleet.

Gile explains that dealerships "aren't going to see cars as much in the future, as manufacturers keep making them more efficient. So, we need to find ways to bring other revenues in-house. Dealerships are drastically changing."

## Coddling Customers

Indeed, the Gile family has shown its devotion to the customer-centric experience in one of the most important ways possible: investment.

Overall, facilities improvements and refinements can make a dramatic difference in creating the customer-centric service experience.

But while an operation like Motorcars is bringing sophisticated technology and great experiences to its facilities to wow and delight customers, making sure your dealership is consumer-centric doesn't have to be over the top or even complicated.

You can make significant progress just by putting on one of those "Customer" hats that we discussed earlier in this book, looking at the facility as customers see it.

For Coleman, this was a simple matter. "I quit looking at the place through the eyes of an employee or the dealer and instead through the eyes of the customer. Every Saturday I would grab a service manager and stroll around the grounds with him. There's a bulb out over there, cigarette butts on the ground over here, and everything else. We're usually blind to all of that because we walk in every day so we aren't seeing what customers see."

The large midwestern dealer group also has been pursuing ways to increase service- capacity throughput while improving the customer experience overall and—like Motorcars—making it more transparent.

It is considering installing separate express-lube lanes at multiple locations for those purposes and already has been building a six-bay addition to one of its stores, in an investment that will total around $2 million.

And while the goal of these bays is to turn over an oil-change customer in 30 minutes or less, each bay will have a hoist in it so that if customers want simple additional "speed-based" services such as tire rotations, they can be accommodated versus having to take the time to move the vehicle into the shop—or at a traditional Jiffy Lube or other quick-change chain that doesn't have hoists,

"Our design will allow us to do simple functions like that and only take an additional seven or eight minutes to do it," the service leader of the large midwestern dealer group says.

"The benefit of installing a lift over the express bay is that we can perform a simple tire rotation or brake inspection in a little as seven to ten minutes."

"If we segment our business that way, we won't be shunning our walk-in business," the service leader says. "We can cut the average time for our non-appointment customers significantly this way.

"We've been focusing on what to do about non-appointment business as well as appointment customers the last couple of years. So, every time there's a building or remodeling project, there's a focus on how do we make ourselves better for all customers.

Interestingly, as it begins another of these installations, this group got some resistance from an OEM that was uncomfortable about the dealership's plans to install hoists. The OE didn't want the customers to be able to view work going on in the express-lube lane.

But they were resolute. They considered extra convenience and process transparency paramount for their customers.

"It's awesome for customers to be able to see what's going on," the service leader says. "And it puts positive pressure on the dealer. If people can see the car, then they need to see something happening. It makes us be better."

After some dialogue, the OEM approved large midwestern dealer group's plans. "And now it's part of our standard set for approaching these remodeling's and our new buildings, and our architects know to always include it," the service leader of the large midwestern dealer group says.

This is a great example of looking through the customer's eyes, re-imagining what the experience *can* be, and taking decisive action to operationalize that vision.

## Lovin' The Lounge

A great way to make customers feel they're at the center of your universe is to pamper them in your waiting area.

Indeed, your primary goal may be to minimize the amount of time that customers have to spend waiting for vehicles. But, as long as they're spending time with you, you can score a lot of points by treating customer really well.

Consider the picture Nicholson paints the waiting experience a service customer will encounter in the lounge at Temecula Hyundai.

"The receptionist begins popping popcorn for the lounge at 7 a.m.," he says. "When you go into a movie theater, the first thing you smell is popcorn, right? Why not create that same, wonderful first smell at our dealership? If a customer has skipped breakfast and needs a little fiber, they will grab a bag of our popcorn even early in the morning.

"So, they put a little something in their stomach, and they can grab a comfortable chair and watch some TV while they wait."

One of the keys is that customers will find that Temecula has really thought through those TVs and chairs, too. The dealership recently trashed its old lounge chairs and got new ones that are "unbelievably comfortable," Nicholson says.

"If we have 14 people waiting here between 8 and 10 in the morning, 10 of those 14 in the chairs will be sound asleep within 15 minutes.

"We started out thinking we would put in recliners, but then we realized, 'Gee, people will want to stay here all day,'" he says with a laugh. "We got just really comfortable, overstuffed chairs that people absolutely love to sit in."

Nicholson put just as much thought into the television situation in the room. Typically, a dealership waiting area may put up one television for waiting customers.

Yet even if it's a 60-inch, 4K job, what's on TV can be problematic if not every customer wants to watch the same program or channel. And in an era of an American public that is divided politically, a tug-of-war between customers who want to watch CNN and those who want to watch Fox News can get pretty lively!

So, Temecula Hyundai has three nice TVs in the waiting lounge tuned to different stations to suit different tastes and interests. It's sort of the sports-bar approach: If you don't want to watch football, well, we also have basketball and hockey.

The dealership waiting lounge and related amenities at Motorcars Honda comprise another reason to think of that dealership as one of the leaders in this nascent discipline of customer-centric auto service.

At Motorcars, leadership put a lot of thought into how to treat customers while they're waiting for their automobiles. One good move: Motorcars tweaked the Daylights Donut recipe and serves them at a little on-premises doughnut shop.

(The doughnuts and other treats are so popular that the Gile family opened Daylight Donuts & Coffee just down the street from the dealership!)

Also, there is a big play area for children that Gile calls the "kids' dealership." It features a 500-gallon aquarium, Lego table, selfie zone and gaming area. "Parents love it, too; I see adults playing in there."

Also, to make both kids and parents feel secure, there is only one way into and out of the area.

"We took things to a different level with this," he says. "If kids aren't having fun, they won't want to come back with their parents, and the parents might think of other ways to have their cars serviced, such as Jiffy Lube."

Gile says that Motorcars wants "customers to feel like they're not in a car dealership but just hanging out in a comfortable atmosphere. If we can make them feel they're not in a traditional service department, time becomes less important."

## Taking Care of Your Team

Some dealers and service leaders are extending their customer-centric operating philosophy to their employee teams.

Take Fletcher Jones. The group has been writing checks for a facility improvement that is solely for the benefit of its employees, because happier employees make for happier customers—a pay-it-back step in the group's customer-centric journey.

At one of its service-center-only locations, the company recently filled out a 350,000-square-foot building with a gym just for the service advisors and 90 technicians at the place. Once targeted to serve as a sales outlet, the building now is outfitted with eight elliptical machines, bicycles, treadmills and free weights, as well as balls and stretch bands, with mirrors, padded floors and showers.

"It's a place where they can get off the service drive and work out," Sweeney says. "Or they can do it after work It's just too hard for them to get away during the day over lunch when they have to go a mile to a gym."

It's costing Fletcher Jones about $40,000 to outfit the pre-existing building, but Sweeney says it'll be worth every penny. "These are the people who take care of your people, your customers," he says. "And when they're in a better place, the experience for the customer is going to be happier."

Meanwhile, Fletcher Jones used another part of the same building to open a lounge for service advisors whose entrance is about 50 feet each from the Audi-service drive and the Mercedes-Benz-service drive. It's got a television, comfortable chairs, a microwave, refrigerator, desktops, and a conference table for meetings and training.

"No dealer wants his service advisors to be sitting at a desk in the service area and eating a sandwich or chips," Sweeney says. "Plus, this offers a bit of escape, off the drive, during the day. Being a service advisor is a high stress job, we expect service advisors to work ungodly hours and this can burn them out. We have to remember that they see more customers than anyone else in the dealership"

We see that investing in facilities, to make them more inviting for customers and for employees, can go a lot way toward making your dealership customer-centric.

And when you do so, don't do it half-heartedly, because you can spend almost as much money outfitting facilities badly as you can doing it well. Make the improvements like the future of your dealership depends on them, because as a customer-centric enterprise—it does.

### Key Takeaways:

- Investing in customer-centric facilities can be a great retention tool.
- Increasingly, consumers want to look "behind the curtain," so consider ways for them to view the service process.
- Consider making your service lounge a comfortable and entertaining part of the customer experience.
- Happy employees create happy customers, so improving amenities and conditions for your personnel can also be worthwhile investments.

While not part of your facilities per se, making it easier and more comfortable for customers to get to and from your service department is another way to show them they're at the center of your thinking— and your operation. We're going to look at that next.

# Chapter 15

Turning Transportation Into A Plus for Customers

Customer transportation to and from the dealership is another area where digital technology is helping service leaders extend their customer-centric operating philosophy. At Temecula Hyundai, for instance, the service department has switched from a fleet of its own shuttle buses to using Lyft to get rides for customers from drop-off at the dealership to home or work.

"Their expectation might be that they're getting a shuttle ride to work," he says. "But would you rather ride in a shuttle with three other people, or just by yourself? Would you rather be late to work because you're the fifth drop-off of five people in the vehicle? What makes more sense as a lean model?"

Meanwhile, Fletcher Jones has a different tack for customer transportation: It's not the dealership's responsibility any more, it's the customer's job. I'm told it's been a win-win situation for both parties—and brought an overall boost in customer satisfaction.

Fletcher Jones Audi sits on the outskirts of downtown Chicago, and of course traffic conditions around there are typically difficult toward the end of the business day—exactly when most customers want to be picked up from their homes or offices, taken to the dealership to get their vehicles and head back out for what might be a busy weekday evening.

The dealership was trying to meet these pickup needs with a fleet of five vans that were on the go all day, and especially during evening rush hour. But it wasn't working.

"The pickup in the evening is where the service would implode," Sweeney tells me. "People would forget about how great a driver was based just on the fact that it would take him 45 minutes to get the customer back to the dealership even though he was only five miles away. The customer had to be at Johnny's soccer game. Nobody would ever say it was a great experience because we can't be everywhere. The best experience we could deliver with these circumstances was a C-plus."

This concern weighed on Sweeney. While few, if any of us, like to be delayed, it's better than likely that a high-end customer such as Audi buyers views "their time is as valuable as their money."

Sweeney and the team came up with a solution: Uber. The service department sends a link to the customer for coordination with Uber when they want to come back. This gives control of the timing of their ride to customers, who no longer are tethered to the schedule of a dealership shuttle driver. In the dense environs of central Chicago, the average time it takes a customer to line up an Uber ride back to the dealership is only about two minutes.

The change also frees service advisors of the stress of arranging shuttle rides and the responsibility for whether the service is performing adequately. And, of course, Fletcher Jones was able to get rid of its shuttle vans and the expense of maintaining and manning them. "It takes stress off both us and the consumer, and the ease of doing business with us increases for them," he says.

Also, Fletcher Jones has been researching the potential installation of service kiosks, which can sit alongside the service lane and allow customers to check in their vehicles for appointments. The principle isn't that different from self-serve ordering kiosks that have been installed at many McDonald's, right next to the traditional order counters.

However, another consideration is to maintain the personal touch, so if Fletcher Jones were to deploy kiosks, it might do so only for prescheduled services such as quick lubes. "But we're trying to get the right first impression of the store, which can skew the whole day just like the last impression. And it may make the day easier for customers if they can just drop off the car and use Uber and leave, and then a service advisor can take over the appointment with Xtime."

You can see the philosophy at work here—a continuous journey to push the envelope and find ways to make it easier for the customer to do business with you, make it a little more convenient, make it a little more intuitive. This is the product of a customer-centric mindset— you're never done.

## Key Takeaways:

- A big inconvenience for customers is getting to and from the dealership for service.
- Get creative in addressing the transportation challenge, maybe providing coupons for Uber or Lyft.

Related to having Facilities to enable the customer-centric experience is having the right Capacity. It's a challenge, but it's very important. That's what we're going to examine in the next chapter.

# Chapter 16

## Flex Your Current Capacity

**L**ack of capacity is the enemy of retention. I've written that exact sentence twice now in this book because it is that important.

Luckily, there are lots of options when it comes to growing  shop capacity. This is important, because recent research suggests additional capacity may be close at hand.

For example, the Cox Automotive 2018 Service Industry Study found that that 86 percent of service bays are currently utilized (for single-shift shops).

But the same study also suggests adding capacity won't necessarily be easy—62 percent of dealer personnel surveyed have concerns about increasing the efficiency of their service processes.

Any capacity-building effort should start with careful consideration of how you load your shop. Are you scheduling appointments tightly and balancing the workload coming into the shop?

It's easy for these two priorities to fall out of balance. When they do, it's a sign that you may need to reconcile appointments with your technician capacity and workflow.

Once you've optimized shop loading, you can pay overtime to handle a temporary bulge in demand. Increasing shift length, adding shifts, and adding weekend hours are also common practices.

Once those are in place, you can consider moving recon out of the shop, either to dedicated techs (maybe on a night shift?) or even outsourcing recon to a third party to make room for more customer work.

I understand the old saw that the used-car department is the service department's best customer. But I don't believe that you should chase away lifetime dollars from good customers for todays used-car business.

There are plenty of options – you can and should have the best of both. Once you're truly customer-centric, the pivot gives you a new perspective to re-assess options.

The final option is always adding bricks and mortar to create capacity. Once you've exhausted all the other options, it's the next logical step. We tend to get anxious about breaking new ground, but if you've already exhausted all the other options to increase capacity and you still have demand … well, as my daughter likes to say, "That sounds like the opposite of a problem."

Here's a good capacity-building example from Temecula Hyundai. The service department has eight stalls and is adding another seven bays behind its pre-existing service facility, about doubling its current service capacity.

Not only that, but Nicholson targeted the area that was occupied by vehicle sales inventory that had been sitting on other space in the back. He persuaded the general manager to rent a storage unit across town and move all the cars there.

So now Temecula Hyundai has service parking for 75 to 80 cars, which will be crucial as Temecula doubles its daily service capacity over its current 117 cars a day.

## Keeping Tabs on Capacity

Sometimes dealers can find ways to create more capacity from the dealership's current footprint and configuration, which, as I noted, is the first option any smart executive would choose.

That's the approach being taken by Del Grande Dealer Group. Williams, the former service director, says, "I live and breathe hours" – capacity considerations are that important to customer satisfaction. "That is all I care about."

He says the dealerships monitor capacity continually. "Every tech is worth nine hours a day, and I need to sell those nine hours every day," he says.

"Yes, I want to make them more efficient, but I want to start with trying to get nine hours out of them every day. Some guys work 12 hours a day and I give them a hug; some guys work six hours a day, and I try to make them more efficient.

"Do they need training? Are they just challenged or lazy? Are there parts not available? I try to take the obstacles out of the way so they're more efficient. Then I have more capacity and can offer more appointments, so customers aren't saying they can't get in for a week."

Similarly, the large midwestern dealer group is trying to figure out how to squeeze more capacity out of current operations. One of their stores has been experimenting with shifts of four 10-hour days to increase utilization of bays by the 27 technicians.

"We took a poll to see if that was something that interested them," the leader of the large midwestern dealer group says. "Some couldn't do it because of family situations and wanted to stay on five-day, eight-hour shifts. But some guys were really excited about it. It gave us the ability to increase capacity in the hours when most people don't like to work."

## Capacity Matters in Parts, Too

Parts availability is one often-overlooked possibility for improving customer satisfaction, and of course that's a material asset that can be affected by facility planning.

While it's not a part of bricks-and-mortar capacity, parts operations are a crucial component of a dealership's functional capacity.

"We have a small parts department," says Muth of Hilton Head Honda. "But parts availability without a doubt affects customer satisfaction. The customer-satisfaction survey will literally ask you if the parts were available for your appointment. And it will ask you if your vehicle was fixed on a first visit.

"If your vehicle is fixed on a first appointment, that one question alone weighs heaviest on the survey. That can mean so many different things. It could mean that my car wasn't fixed properly on the first visit because the technician forgot to reset the maintenance light; but they can mark you '0' for that.

"They can say that my car wasn't fixed right the first visit because a part wasn't in stock. So, yes, without a doubt, it means a lot to have parts in stock, parts on hand, or to be able to get them in a decent amount of time to fix these vehicles."

The leader of the large midwestern dealer group says that even their high expectations of parts availability are one way in which modern consumers are placing more expectations on automotive service departments. Maybe they've just become so used to next-day delivery from some Amazon super-warehouse 100 miles away that they apply the same standards to every commercial transaction.

"Customers used to give you so much more time back in the day, in terms of expecting that their car was going to be in the shop all day," the leader of the large midwestern dealer group says. "But today, in many of our stores, 60 percent or more of our customers are either no-appointments or no-waiting. And so, if you don't have those parts in stock, it just causes a lot of frustration, and [customers] don't want to have to come back. They want to get in and out the first time.

"We find that, as a group, there's pretty close to that dollar-for-dollar ratio between parts and service sales. So, if we're generating more parts sales or, vice versa, more service sales, that does help the whole operation."

At Vaden Automotive Group, Newsome finds that "parts availability has a huge impact on customer satisfaction. Some of it is just customers' perception of being able to get their cars fixed the same day or being able to get them fixed the first time.

"Some customers perceive coming back for a part that's ordered as a second trip, that they didn't fix it right the first time. So, that's huge."

When dealerships decide to become truly customer-centric, it calls for utilizing their multi-million-dollar investment in facilities in new ways.

### Key Takeaways:

- You can't frustrate customers due to lack of service times, so manage capacity to ensure availability.
- There are many ways to flex capacity.
- Parts availability is an important part of being customer-centric.

Congratulations if you've addressed every part of the Outer Circle and the Inner Circle in our model of a customer-centric dealership.

Now we've got to help you understand and measure why things are getting better, so that you can keep improving. And that means adopting new metrics, while de-emphasizing some of the industry's traditional measures of customer satisfaction.

# Chapter 17

Critical KPIs for a Customer-Centric Dealership

**W**e've discussed all of those important elements in the Outer Circle for building a customer-centric dealership: Leadership, Culture, People, Technology, Facilities and Capacity.

We've also given you lots to think about for how to apply some of the important elements of that Inner Circle—Tools and Processes, Marketing, Training and Scheduling – to your goal of becoming a customer-centric enterprise.

Let's move on to the next step—measuring progress toward your goal, and how quickly you're making that progress.

To do this correctly, you'll need to go beyond the traditional metrics that we've long used to measure customer satisfaction. You'll need Key Performance Indicators (KPIs) that actually indicate if you're making headway as you break to a more customer-centric operating philosophy.

Some might question whether new KPIs or metrics are necessary. But I would suggest that you consider how much traditional measures, such as service absorption and hours per RO, really tell you about the experience you're delivering. Let's remember: Hours per RO is a transaction-centric metric that tells you if you're selling work, but doesn't assess whether customers needed it, or they're happy with it.

The risk, of course, is that focusing solely on traditional metrics can undermine your ability to deliver a great overall experience with every customer.

"We chase these numbers, but behind all of this is a real experience that has to happen," says Vince Sweeney, who oversees service departments for Fletcher Jones dealerships. "We push our guys so hard to get CSI numbers, they're in fear of taking care of customers."

Fortunately, Sweeney notes, some manufacturers finally are veering away from the traditional customer satisfaction measurements in favor of new assessments that focus on customer retention and loyalty.

For your dealership, you don't need to wait for OEMs to change their minds about customer satisfaction measures before you tailor your own information gathering for a customer-centric approach.

In fact, if you want to measure the right things to help move the organization in that direction, you'll need to put new metrics in place.

You know the old adage: "You can't manage it if you can't measure it." Sure, your dealership needs a good score. But at the end of the day, who wants "satisfied" customers who don't come back?

As the service-technology leader Les Silver has said,

---

*"Satisfaction is necessary, but it's not sufficient. The goal is retention."*

---

Your objective is customer loyalty, and satisfaction is only one component of loyalty.

How will you know how well you're doing in becoming customer-centric?

As mentioned, I've purposely stayed away from traditional service department metrics, such as absorption, and from anything else that may be related to a transaction-centric framework. These are already well understood, and in some cases are becoming less relevant as our industry changes.

Instead, you must determine and set some numerical targets that both will achieve significant improvement for your dealership in important operational efficiencies – and, more important, signal reliably that you are on your way to becoming a truly customer-centric dealership.

Here are some ideas for new-era KPIs and a discussion of my reasoning in selecting each:

## Retention:

Those of you who read *Fast Lane* may recall that I believe the time has come for the retail automotive industry to rethink what service retention should mean for dealers and their OEM partners.

I advocate a longer view of retention, one that would encourage all of us to think more broadly about the scope of service work we could and should retain over time.

Let's redefine service retention as the vehicle owner returning to you for *everything*—maintenance, repairs, recalls, state inspections, appearance enhancements and so on.

Define the potential service visits  for every individual vehicle, and then measure the actual as compared to the potential. This has several advantages, the primary ones being that we'd know exactly how well we're doing, and this definition of retention could be applied universally to all vehicles.

We could have a single measure for the industry to work from, versus the patchwork of definitions of retention that exists today.

Unfortunately, this description of retention is just a theory today. It would take some collective effort from the largest players in the business to make it a reality.

In the meantime, we'll need to rely on the various measurements that are already in place from your OEMs and/or technology-system vendors. The important thing today is that you a) understand the various metrics available to you, pick the best from the ones available, establish a baseline and track it over time to see how your efforts are affecting your retention.

In that regard, one metric I like a lot is average number of visits per year, per customer (AVY). The frequency of customer visits would be a good indicator of how well you're doing in retaining and engaging with your customers.

In my experience, a reasonable target for this metric is 1.5 times per year. It seems reasonable given the number of potential reasons for customers to visit, including maintenance recommendations, multi-point safety inspections, recalls, repairs and, where they're applicable, the requirement for state inspections of vehicles.

Over time as your operation becomes more customer-centric and your customer loyalty increases, your AVY should go up as well.

## Capacity:

Lack of capacity hurts retention. You need to be able to accommodate customers with emergency situations immediately, and regular maintenance and repair work within two days of the request.

Your appointment-scheduling system should be set up to reflect your capacity, and its reporting capabilities should be able to tell you how far out you're booking. Accommodate maintenance and repair customers within two days and emergencies immediately.

Ensure that you're examining specific areas of the shop for bottlenecks in addition to looking at averages.

## Selling Philosophy:

It's worth repeating that the days of slamming huge ROs on customers are gone. Optimizing the RO for today will chase away the customer forever—so take the long-term view.

Only sell what the factory recommends or what fixes an immediate and real problem. Not only review your reports to see the top 10 things being sold, also look at the top 10 things being *recommended by your advisors*. Unnecessary recommendations, even if unsold, damage your credibility.

## Service Appointments:

Because appointment customers generally have a better experience, their service retention is 7.5 percent higher.[7] Given this, target an 85-percent appointment-to-walk-in ratio. I'd also recommend aiming to secure at least 50 percent of your appointments from your digital scheduling tools.

## Service Lane:

All customers should be greeted and acknowledged immediately. Target time to complete the write-up for appointment customers should be less than five minutes, and less than ten minutes for walk-in customers.

You must have mobile technology in the service lane to enable your team to get away from the desks and podiums to get to the customer quickly.

## Vehicle Service Time:

As we've already discussed, consumers who are most satisfied spend 2.5 hours or less getting their vehicle serviced. Consumers who are in for service 2.4 hours or less say they're "very satisfied, I'll always go to them" (the dealer).

[7] Source: Xtime, based on dealers with Go-Live date before September 1, 2016, OEM-specific vehicles only, Dec ember 2016 – November 2017.

When the time increases to three hours, the vehicle owner states, "Somewhat satisfied, I might use in the future." When you get to 3.7 hours or beyond, the sentiment degrades to "very dissatisfied, I'll never go back."

Two of the top five frustrations consumers have with dealers are related to time spent waiting, with 30 percent frustrated that the service took longer than expected, and 13 percent unhappy because they had an appointment and still had to wait in line.[8]

## Inspections:

As vehicles become increasingly complex, providing consumers assurance as to the status of their repair also increases in importance. Accordingly, the objective for the MPI is that 100 percent of vehicles should have an inspection report delivered to the customer. "No Inspection Needed" should be a rarity (less than 10 percent.) All completed inspections should generate an inspection report that is delivered to the customer. And the declined services data from the MPI reports should be mined for follow-up outreach.

## Sales-to-Service Handoff:

Research shows that only 41 percent of customers are introduced to the service department at the time of purchase, but 53 percent say that the handoff comes into play when they decide where to repair the vehicle.

Your objective here should be at least 80 percent, and of course a great showing would be 100 percent. And there's just no good reason that you can't achieve such a handoff every time.

The best practice is not only to do the service walk-through but set the first service appointment in conjunction with the service handoff.

Since this is very important, let me say again that people will behave in the way that their pay plan encourages them—so consider if you need to use pay-plan adjustments to drive this behavior.

## Tech Efficiency:

Many service managers tell me that they estimate their techs actually work on vehicles only 50 percent of the time they're in the shop!

[8] Source: Cox Automotive 2018 Service Industry Study.

So, while current work-tracking systems show technicians as "assigned" one or more ROs, they're actually doing things other than working on the vehicle during those designated periods.

To make sure tech efficiency is an accurate metric you can reliably use, you need ways to keep distractions away from your technicians so that they will keep turning wrenches. The more this roughly 50 percent time wastage can be reduced, the more we will minimize the tech shortage and problems which stem from that.

The reason tech efficiency is important in this discussion is because of its direct impact on capacity – the more technician time spent completing vehicles, the higher your throughput and the more capacity you'll have in your shop. Some good ideas include parts runners and point-to-point communication devices between techs and advisors and/or parts personnel.

## Track Online Reviews

Many service managers now say that quantitative and qualitative feedback on social media is at least as important a "metric" as anything else, on digital platforms such as DealerRater.

"We look at our online reputation as most important," says Gile, whose Motorcars Group dealerships in metro Cleveland were rated for four consecutive years as one of the best dealership experiences in Ohio.

"Those speak more than anything else. We get extremes both positive and negative, and they're from the customer so you can't ignore them.

Online reviews also encourage employee engagement with customers, Gile explains, because if they get strong customer evaluations by name, other customers are more likely to ask for them for their own service appointments."

Fletcher Jones retention-loyalty stands at 67 percent, in part because they pay such close attention to what's being said about the dealerships, service departments and the experience in online reviews.

"How do you keep the customers that don't have the best experience?" Sweeney says. "We focus on Prime reviews [on Amazon]. If their experience wasn't good, it comes back to us. Now we're calling the customer before they can kill us on other social media.

"We're not perfect. We're going to make mistakes. It might take too long to get your car back, or it's not as clean as you think it should be. But what we focus on is the ability to turn that around and keep that customer."

Today, there's no excuse for a dealer and service-department manager not to know how their operation is performing in the KPIs that will truly track their progress to a customer-centric enterprise. They've just got to make up their minds to measure them.

### Key Takeaways:

- To progress toward becoming a customer-centric dealership, you need to measure the things that truly indicate your current state – and where you're headed.
- Focus on the numbers that describe these key areas: Retention, Capacity, Selling Philosophy, Service Appointments, Service Lane, Vehicle Service Time, Inspections, Sales-to-Service Handoff, and Tech Efficiency.
- Track and respond to social-media evaluations of your dealership. They can carry a lot of weight with customers.

We've given you a comprehensive, honest, helpful look at what it will take for your dealership to pivot to become truly customer-centric and ensure your long-term prosperity.

Let's take a few minutes to talk about the future.

# Chapter 18

## The Future Is Now

W e've discussed all of those important elements in the Outer Circle for building a customer-centric dealership: Leadership, Culture, People, Technology, Facilities and Capacity.

The automotive industry is in a time of rapid change, and therefore lots of uncertainty. As I've traveled around North America talking to many of you, I'd say there are two types of leaders right now. Let's call them "Uh-Oh" and "Hmm."

Uh-Oh sees that we are in the midst of rapid change and is taking immediate steps to navigate to the future. Hmm has a feeling that something is going on, is hearing lots of dire talk from his peers and maybe the industry press but wants to wait and see how "things play out."

If you haven't already, I urge you to join the Uh-Oh team. Despite the uncertainty, we need to act with urgency on multiple fronts for the future of your fixed operations.

With around 270 million gasoline-powered vehicles on the roads, and with vehicles increasing in complexity, we all understand that there's no immediate danger of opening the service drive on Monday morning and no one being there.

The danger is that you don't do the groundwork now, so when the stuff starts to hit the fan you're unprepared.

Consider what is happening as we speak to fixed-ops revenue and margins: Today's vehicles have lengthening maintenance intervals, so they need less service. Over-the-air software updates are eliminating that need to visit the dealership. Improving quality overall means less repair and recall volumes will probably drop (assuming no more large-scale campaigns like Takata or bad ignition switches).

Electrical components are replacing mechanical—again, less repair work needed. We're seeing more sensors on vehicles, so fewer accidents. Longer term, electric vehicles have 70 percent fewer moving parts on average, so the service revenue potential is significantly less.

And the competition (old and new) isn't sitting still. They are strategizing, acting and investing to keep the customers that they have—and to take even more away from you.

This book offers a lot of ways for dealers and service leaders to adopt a customer-centric operating philosophy as a primary means to serve and retain a larger share of customers to drive profitable growth. The potential is there: Today, dealers get about 33 percent of all service visits in the U.S.[9] That means we have 67-percent upside if we can convince customers who have defected to return to us.

The obvious way to do this is to pivot to customer-centricity—build the organization outlined in the Outer Circle and Inner Circle I described; be the organization that delivers that technology-enhanced experience—and some of that 67 percent will come to you *very soon*.

## Back to the Future

But how does that take care of the future?

Here's one of the beautiful things about being customer-centric. If you own the customer relationship—I mean really own the customer relationship—then most of the future is already in the bag. You will get an increasing share of the remaining 67 percent, which will offset the maintenance intervals, improved quality and reduced recalls. And don't forget, loyal customers buy more often, at a higher margin, and send you referrals.

---

*Loyal customers buy more often, at a higher margin, and send you referrals.*

---

Longer term, you'll get more than your share of EV sales, and the wiper, tire, brake and other business that will come with it.

Subscription business becomes popular? Great—they'll come to you to subscribe, and the subscription business has built-in loyalty; the service business is usually bundled with the monthly subscription.

Advantage: dealer.

Over time, you'll evolve into being the local transportation-solution provider—regardless of where the automotive industry goes—because you have the customer.

[9] Source: Cox Automotive 2018 Service Industry Study.

Of course, you have to do more than become customer-centric to really mitigate margin compression in fixed ops. We must find ways to improve operational efficiencies using new technologies and tools.

When I say to improve operational efficiencies, generally I mean doing more while reducing your costs, handling more transactions with fewer people, or with less-expensive people.

There are several ways that new technology can help you achieve these objectives. Notable examples include improving your service-lane efficiency with mobile devices and enabling your service advisors to text with customers so they're not chasing them on the phone. Provide your customers the ability to pay online so you can reduce the load at the cashier.

As I mentioned earlier, most of the service leaders I speak to say that their techs only spend about 50 percent of their time actually working on vehicles. The rest is wasted time. To get to the bottom of this requires direct observation, because your DMS dispatching module probably reports 100 percent utilization. Of course, this just means the tech has one (or more) ROs assigned; it doesn't mean they're actually working on the vehicle.

Keeping the techs in the bay is very important. Improve your shop loading so that you have a good balance of express, repair and maintenance, provide them an automated MPI tool.

What other areas can you focus on? Here are some ideas that I believe will be very important to drive customer-centricity and/or help mitigate revenue decline and margin compression.

## Tires

I get that tires don't have much margin and can be a headache, but tires are also an incredible opportunity. Passenger-car and passenger-light-truck tire-replacement sales were approximately $30 billion in 2016, with dealers picking up only 8.5 percent of that opportunity.[10]

While we have increased our share from 7 percent in 2012, we still have a lot of work to do. Here are some sobering and compelling statistics:[11]

[10] Source: *Modern Tire Dealer* magazine.
[11] Ibid.

- 16 percent of vehicles that come through the service drive need tires.
- 78 percent of customers buy tires from the first person to recommend based on need.
- 75 percent have their vehicle serviced where tires are purchased.
- 13 percent of tire sales include alignment.

Tires are the Number One reason a customer will shop outside the dealer network—tires help drive customer retention. And 78 percent of tire customers are repeat buyers (from the same retail location each time).[12]

There are many reasons to get into tire sales. By becoming a "one-stop shop" you are making it more convenient for the customer. You are also blocking the competition by eliminating a defection point.

Of course, selling tires leads to selling additional higher-margin services such as brakes, alignments, suspension repairs, and more. Companies like DealerTire make it relatively easy to get into the tire business, and you can turbocharge your tire business by including tires in your technologies that manage your service marketing, service lane and MPI's.

## Accessories

Accessories can drive big gains in service, sales or both. Consider that the accessories market is $41 billion, is growing 4 percent annually and enjoying a 40-percent to 48-percent gross margin. Six million new vehicles are accessorized in the first two years of ownership, more than 80 percent in the first 120 days.

The typical spend: $300 to $800, while the truck spend averages $1,500! And 33 percent of specialty-equipment consumers are under 30 years old. Unfortunately, dealers only hold an 8 percent share of this market.

The gold standard for accessory sales is Galpin Motors in Southern California, where 50 percent of new vehicles sold are equipped with

---

[12] Michelin data.

new or aftermarket accessories. They contribute a significant margin enhancement, typically 40 percent to 50 percent on the equipment.[13]

On the service side, consider the example of Findlay Toyota in Nevada. They took the bold step of removing their Express Lube and installing an accessory showroom for service customers. This boosted fixed-ops revenue an average of $500,000 per store.

Of course, there are challenges to capturing more accessory business, including stocking proper inventory and financing. But there are vendors out there who provide software and expertise to overcome these challenges, and the upside is very attractive.

Getting into the vehicle-personalization business can have an immediate benefit now, and in the future when ownership moves toward fleet management, you'll have the customer connection and relationship to serve those needs.

## Pick-up/Drop-off

The distance customers are willing to drive for service seems to be shrinking. I suppose that's not too surprising in this era of same-day delivery and the coming-soon, "A drone will drop it in your backyard."

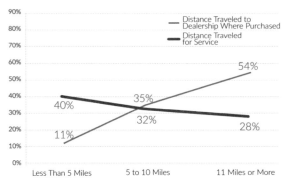

**Distance Traveled by Consumers**

Source: 2018 Cox Automotive Service Industry Study

Interestingly, recent research shows that consumers are willing to drive greater distances to save money on a vehicle purchase, but only 28 percent are willing to drive more than 11 miles for service.

[13] Sources: Automotive News, Fixed Ops Journal, 2018 Auto Accessories Trend Report.

One of the pioneers of pick-up/drop-off is Witt Lincoln in San Diego. They have a network of 10 drivers and they operate in a similar fashion to Uber; they use a tracking app and their appointment-scheduling system allows customers to make appointments for the valet service. They've even embedded a link to pick-up/drop-off in their service reminders emails—which explains their whopping 35 percent response rate. Not only do they pick-up and return the vehicle, they also provide a loaner vehicle for the customer to use while the vehicle is being serviced.

---

*You must either get the vehicle to your service, or your service to the vehicle.*

---

Service Director Scott Witt tells me that the service "has been fun" and "the customers love it." Seventy-five to 80 percent of our valet customers are under warranty," Witt says. "Our drivers use the app for tracking, and we even take pictures of the vehicle condition before and after drop-off."

Witt began providing the service to their customers about ten years ago, and since then the Lincoln Motor Company has begun providing the service; currently its offered to 2016 and newer vehicles as part of the overall Lincoln warranty, so Lincoln subsidizes a good portion of the service. "We're very lucky to have a partner that is so forward thinking," says Witt.

He tells me the majority of customers are in the one- to 30-mile range from the dealership, with 45 percent to 50 percent of total users over 20 miles from the dealership. They even have customers who use the service that are 30 to 50 miles from the dealership. Witt is certain that these customers wouldn't be retained without the valet service.

He says the service is a fantastic tool for retention, with 98 percent of surveys rating the service "very pleased"—the highest rating. He also reports valet customers have a tendency to spend more.

The need is stark: You must either get the vehicle to your service, or your service to the vehicle.

## Car Washes

In the past, we all thought of car washing as a "necessary evil." But now there's developing school of thought that car washes also can be great for loyalty *and* a significant source of new revenue.

I've discussed the Motorcars Dealer Group from Cleveland previously, particularly the LOF conveyor belt. The Gile family has pioneered many unique customer-experience enhancements— and once again they're re-thinking the status quo.

First, they moved the service department's car wash to a dedicated building—that creates more service bays—and invested in car washes that can do more than 100 vehicles per hour yet require only two to three employees per shift.

Motorcars gives all service customers coupons for a wash *gratis*, which frees up valets and other dealership resources. Because of the high throughput and low labor costs, the Giles can add new and even larger car washes every three years. They report that customers love it, and more than 70 percent of customers using the wash have never been to either of their dealerships. Motorcars also can grow brand recognition for their stores with consumers who own competitive brands.

Still not sure you want to pivot to create a truly customer-centric dealership? OK, here's the million-dollar question (literally): what's the alternative? Hope that it all works out, that the world stops changing? Or maybe consumer trends (especially among coming generations) suddenly head in a different direction?

Maybe your OEM will come up with a new type of vehicle, one so much better than anything else on the market that consumers will line up to have one, and it'll be just like the good old days?

Are you kidding?

There's no alternative, unless you're planning on exiting the business. And I'm going to assume that since you've invested the time to read this book, that's not your plan.

It seems inescapable to me: The best option is to place that customer in the center and deliver a world-class, technology-enhanced service experience, where each element of customer-centricity is optimized, enabling us to capture more of that 67 percent of service visits not coming to the dealership—today and tomorrow.

I believe this is the key strategy for dealers to lay the foundation for continued prosperity. It's my sincere hope that this book helps you focus on the customer and secure the future—no matter where it leads us.

Jim Roche, December 6, 2018.

# Epilogue

## Tackling the Transparency/Trust Problem

Much of Fast Break focuses on how dealers can implement a technology-enhanced experience to retain a larger share of their service customers.

But as 2019 comes to a close, and a new decade dawns, it's become clear that providing a technology-enhanced experience, in and of itself, may not be enough for dealers to achieve the level of loyalty and trust that consumers expect to keep them coming back.

How can this be, you may ask?

The answer, I believe, lies in between the lines of what we already know, and what we're learning, about the things that shape trust among today's consumers.

Let's start with what might be considered an obvious point—that today's consumers actually want to trust dealers and their service teams.

In 2019, Cox Automotive's Technology and Transformation of Retail Study found that 62 percent of respondents want to regard the individuals who help service their vehicles as an "advisor, mentor, partner or friend."

**62%**

Want a more trusting relationship with the dealer - like an **Advisor, Mentor, Partner or Friend**

Source: Cox Automotive 2019 Technology & Transformation of Retail Study

When I first saw this take-away on trust, it was a head-scratcher.

I thought of the hundreds, if not thousands, of dealerships where leaders *have* made a concerted effort to provide a better, technology-enhanced customer experience in their service departments. I thought of the hours and hours of training service advisors have received to engage customers in a more consultative, meaningful way.

If all this good stuff is happening, why are nearly two-thirds of today's consumers effectively saying that all these positive, ostensibly trust-building efforts by dealers and service department leaders are falling short? Wouldn't it be reasonable to believe that, if dealers really were doing the good job I've thought they were doing, the percentage of consumers who sought more trust from their dealership service department would be significantly smaller?

All this thinking led to an epiphany that goes something like this:

While dealers are providing a better experience, loyalty isn't improving.

### Share of Service Visits By Vehicle Age
Among those who purchased from a dealership

62%   < 2-year-old vehicles

56%   < 2 to 5-year-old vehicles

> 5-year-old vehicles   29%

### Top Reasons to Not Use Dealer for Service
- Total cost unreasonable
- Inconvenient location
- They'll overcharge me
- Unreasonable labor $$
- Unreasonable parts $$

Of the top five reasons consumers defect from dealer service, four have to do with service pricing.

But - dealer prices for maintenance and common services are at parity with the service aftermarket.

### What Are Consumers Paying?
### Oil Change Snapshot

| Retail Auto Service | Quick Lube | Dealership Where Purchased | Tire Store/ Repair Chain | General Repair Service Station |
|---|---|---|---|---|
| $58 | $60 | $61 | $75 | $77 |

Source: Cox Automotive 2018 Service Industry Study

As I considered these findings together, it made me think that dealers and their service departments may not be getting a fair shake from consumers.

After all, if dealers are providing a better experience <u>and</u> if dealer prices are fair and reasonable, then why aren't dealers getting credit for it by increased customer loyalty?

Part of the answer to this question lies, of course, in the transaction-based mindset many dealers and service department leaders have followed over the years.

We know, for example, that dealership service customers specifically cite unreasonable total cost, overcharging and unanticipated labor or parts charges as reasons for defecting, according to the 2018 Cox Automotive Service Industry Study.

If a customer comes in and expects to pay a fair and reasonable price for their 30,000-mile service, and then they get a call with a $800 laundry list of "needed items" I think we can reasonably see how that could break down trust.

As stated earlier, "only sell what the factory recommends or what fixes an immediate and real problem."

But what about dealers who have moved past the transaction-based mindset, and have committed themselves to providing service customers the experience they really want? Why are these dealers also struggling to gain the trust of their service customers and keep them coming back as loyal clients?

The answer, I believe, is that all dealers, no matter the level of customer service excellence they provide, suffer from an awareness and trust problem.

Let's consider the primary reasons consumers get turned off by dealers' service departments.

As we noted earlier, the 2018 Cox Automotive Service Industry study found that four of the top five reasons consumers don't return to dealership service department relates to their pricing.

In short, consumers think dealers and their service departments will over-charge them, even if a dealer's prices are the same, or even less, than those charged by independent and chain service centers.

As I've studied this issue, it's become clear that this level of pricing dissatisfaction offers an opportunity for dealers.

Let's break down the opportunity.

We know, for example, that consumers care deeply about getting vehicle service prices before they come to a dealership.

A 2016 study by Xtime found that 71 percent of consumers want a cost estimate when they set a service appointment—a far bigger priority than having a choice of advisors, appointment times or transportation options.

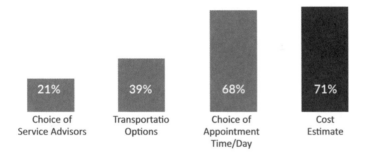

| 21% | 39% | 68% | 71% |
| Choice of Service Advisors | Transportatio Options | Choice of Appointment Time/Day | Cost Estimate |

The interest among consumers about the cost of vehicle repairs shouldn't be a surprise – in today's internet environment, consumers expect at a minimum to know three things if they're going to transact online: tell me what I need, when can I get it and *what does it cost?*

Dealer service is no different, and therein lies a big opportunity.

For example, we see roughly 50 percent of dealers today offer service prices online.

But, if you dig deeper, we see that most dealers who tell the world about their service prices, only post <u>some</u> prices online. Dealers typically aren't as comprehensive about publishing service pricing as they should be, and few seem to be actively marketing their prices as a means of conveying transparency and building trust.

Such lack of attention to pricing allows *the myth* that dealers overcharge for vehicle service to live on, much to the detriment of your service operation.

Given these dynamics, it's no wonder that the single largest point of service customer defection from dealers typically occurs three years after a vehicle purchase, when manufacturer warranties usually end.

The conventional wisdom among dealers and service department leaders is that this defection occurs because customers now understand the cost of any vehicle repairs and service comes out of their pocket.

But what if service customers had a full understanding of what those maintenance and service costs might be *before* their manufacturer warranty ended? Wouldn't it be reasonable to expect that dealers who were fully transparent about their vehicle service costs, and provided a superior, technology-enhanced service experience, stand to retain a larger share of customers after the warranty runs out?

These are somewhat hypothetical questions, but I think we can all agree that dealers would be in a far better position to keep customers for longer periods of their vehicle ownership if dealers made pricing transparency a higher priority.

*You must provide price transparency from the start.*

## Two Paths to Building Transparency and Trust

I've shared my belief that dealers would attract and keep more customers by embracing service pricing transparency in conversations with dealers around the country.

I'll often get the same push-back in these discussions: "That's great, Jim. But if I post my service prices, I'll just get shopped and customers will go somewhere else."

May I share how much I dislike this comment? It's really a reflection of a "throw up your hands and give up" way of thinking.

But the comment contains a nugget of truth.

The truth is that price-minded consumers will shop around to satisfy their desire to know the cost of a particular vehicle repair or service, and they want to know if a specific price represents a fair value for the work needed.

Herein lies another trust-building opportunity for dealers—helping potential service customers understand how your prices compare to the competition.

I view this as an opportunity because, for the most part, there isn't an easy way for customers seeking vehicle service options to find out how one dealer or independent service provider's compare to the other.

In fact, the dearth of a single source for comparative, competitive vehicle service pricing explains why 63 percent of consumers say they would be "likely" or "very likely" to use a trusted website to get answers, and prices, for service, repair or maintenance-related issues, according to 2019 Kelley Blue Book research.

This finding also explains why some third-party websites are looking to fill the void with price-minded service customers.

If you think about it, the absence of prominent third-party resources for vehicle service pricing is a bit surprising.

In every walk of life, there are examples of how third parties help to build trust: commercial negotiators for mergers and acquisitions, relationship mediators for our personal lives or in politics neutral 3rd party countries who mediate peace discussions.

The key is a trusted third party who can bring an individual or group together, present new facts, and help evolve the relationship in a positive direction.

In my view, a third-party presence for vehicle service pricing could be a positive for dealers. It could serve as the proverbial bridge that brings dealers who are embracing price transparency, and providing the positive technology-enhanced experiences consumers want, together with consumers who seek a more advisory, mentor- and partner-like relationship when they get their vehicle repaired or serviced.

What does this proverbial bridge look like? The bridge is a third party, much in the same way that third parties have historically operated in vehicle sales to assist consumers and dealers to come together for vehicle purchases. The trusted third parties for vehicle sales bring pricing expertise and deliver price recommendations to consumers so they have a starting point for discussions with the dealer.

The trusted third party for auto service will operate in a similar way – they'll analyze common services such as oil changes, brakes and tires and develop average price ranges which they'll deliver to consumers.

Let me be clear: I do not think the third-party services will find success if they detail specific dealer prices for service. I can see where this might be a non-starter for dealers and service department leaders. Likewise, I think consumers would be satisfied by knowing average price ranges rather than specifics.

The sites can find success in the same way they've found success with vehicle purchase prices—by working to educate vehicle owners in a manner that creates a starting point for a detailed discussion with the service advisor.

Some might point out that there are currently a few third-party sites that have attempted to offer a repository of pricing information for consumers.

I would concede the point, and counter that none of the entities came with the backing of a trusted brand. If consumers don't trust the information then we're not going to create trust out of thin air.

I'd offer two other considerations:

**Expertise**: It requires resources and sophistication to obtain enough data (hundreds of millions of RO's) to analyze all of the possible combinations of year, make and models, the various services for each and then factor in local labor and other cost factors to <u>deliver correct dealer service price recommendations</u>.

**Audience size**: If a third party doesn't have a brand that has millions of visitors, then having the first two is irrelevant because not enough consumers will ever see it to move the needle for you.

It'll be interesting to see how the third-party efforts play out. We know, for example, that millions of consumers already use other services such as HomeAdvisor.com, which is very similar to automotive in that home repair is infrequent and sometimes complicated and expensive, or Yelp and other recommendation engines for just about every possible need or question.

Given this, it's not surprising that nearly half of consumers show interest in a single, centralized website comparing prices for nearby service departments so they can make the most cost-effective choice, according to the 2018 Cox Automotive Service Industry Study.

## Consumer Interest in Website Feature or Concept

**70%** of consumers want to view price ranges for various services

**41%** of consumers want a website comparing prices for nearby service departments

Based on average dealer service pricing, a trusted third-party tool will guide consumers through the research process and then match them with a dealer who is both close to their location and fair in price.

This transparency leads to increased trust between the service department and consumer, ultimately improving retention rates by giving customers more confidence and trust in the dealer they choose, and the prices they would pay for vehicle repairs and service.

Now, it's also true that dealers could work to bridge the trust gap between themselves and their customers without the help of a third party—just as some dealers do with their new and used vehicle pricing and sales.

The advantage of a Do-It-Yourself (DIY) strategy is that you're the architect and you're in charge, and you'd have the same basic guidelines and priorities as a third-party provider.

First, (no surprise) you'd need to get your prices published. At a minimum, your prices should be published on your website, in your appointment scheduler and displayed in the service lane.

Second, you'd want to hire a company to do local competitive analysis every quarter and publish how your prices compare to the competition (include the source and dates of the analysis).

Third, you'd need to ensure your dealer website is optimized for search engines so that service customers can find you through Google and other portals.

Finally, your SEM strategy should include a budget and plans to optimize your outreach against the searches/keywords that will help drive potential customers to your service scheduling tool.

What are the desired outcomes of third-party or DIY?

In either case, the obvious goal would be more service revenue, which per NADA has an average gross profit of 46 percent, at a time when margins in variable operations are ever-smaller.

In addition, more service customers would help your dealership achieve the strategic objective of increasing vehicle sales. The 2018 Cox Automotive Service Industry Study found that 74 percent of consumers are likely to purchase their next vehicle from your dealership if they returned for service in the last 12 months, as compared to only 35 percent who did not.

## Likely to Return to **Dealer** for Next Vehicle Purchase

**74%**
of those who
RETURNED
for service within the
past 12 months

**VS**

**35%**
of those who
DID NOT
return for service within
the past 12 months

## Why the Time is Now for Transparency, Trust

As I've noted throughout the book, the future prosperity and success of dealerships will increasingly depend on each dealer's ability to improve its service customer loyalty and retention, and reduce the loss of customers to independent and chain service outlets.

To date, the forces of the market and dealer responses to them, would seem to be working in favor of the service providers who serve the customers franchise dealers seem to lose.

But let's remember: Vehicles are getting more technically complex, and consumers are very aware of this, mostly due to media reporting of the future of EV's and AV's. The typical vehicle today has 30-

50 onboard computers, dozens of internal and external sensors and dozens of potential dashboard warnings.

Because of this increasing complexity, consumers are inclined to want to return to the dealer because they assume a higher level of expertise from the business that initially sold them the product. In fact, when it comes to vehicles with advanced vehicle technology, consumers prefer the dealer almost two to one.

## Consumer Preference for Dealers is Higher Among Those with Advanced Features in Their Vehicles

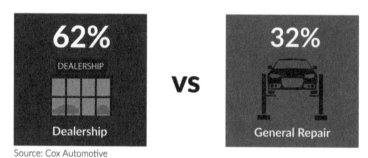

Source: Cox Automotive

How do we capitalize on this consumer sentiment of favoring the dealer? The effect of consumer awareness of vehicle complexity causes confusion and eventually anxiety for the vehicle owner, since a car is typically the second largest investment most consumers ever make. But if you scrape away the histrionics, consumers want to know 4 fundamental things:

- What do I need to do?
- When do I need to do it?
- Who can do it for me?
- About what should it cost

Delivering the answers to these questions positions the dealer to improve trust as well as the opportunity to deliver a convenient, technology enhanced experience that optimizes the opportunity to retain (or re-obtain) the customer.

Today, the conditions are right for dealers to win, and keep, a larger share of the service work that will need to be done.

But dealers won't successfully win this business if they overlook the customer experience as they're working to improve awareness and trust.

The optimal customer experience starts when consumers have landed on your dealership, understand your prices are competitive and your customer experience appears to fit their preferences.

At that point, the next step and consideration for consumers prior to visiting the dealership is scheduling their appointments.

According to the 2018 Cox Automotive Service Industry Study, consumers ultimately want ease and convenience when it comes to scheduling service.

The same study found 56 percent of consumers would choose a dealership that provided online service appointment scheduling over one that didn't offer the option. Also, added amenities like loaner cars, Wi-Fi and dealer ratings are a bonus for consumers while selecting their service provider.

## 56%
of car owners are more likely to service a vehicle at a dealership that offers online scheduling

Source: 2018 Cox Automotive 2018 Service Industry Study

No matter what online service scheduling tool you utilize, it's important to recognize that convenience is perhaps the single-most important priority for consumers.

The process should be simple and user-friendly. Don't make the customer fumble around and try to find a phone number to call you and avoid imposing a cumbersome, many-step scheduling process. If finding and navigating scheduling is difficult, dealerships risk losing this customer to the easy to find local repair shop down the road.

The optimal scheduling process will also ensure that customers can transfer information about their vehicle to service advisors before even driving to the service lane, reducing the time it takes staff to write the customer up and perform an initial inspection of the vehicle.

In addition to improving convenience and efficiency, this process also helps dealers meet rising customer expectations. Nearly nine out of 10 vehicle owners expect the service department to know something about them when they arrive for service, according to the 2019 Cox Automotive Technology and Transformation of Retail Study.

By easing the scheduling process, consumers are more likely to revisit your service department thanks to increased convenience and a more streamlined customer experience.

I know that there are naysayers among you, those that don't want to change or believe you "don't have to play that game."

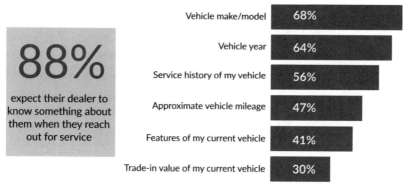

Source: 2019 Cox Automotive Technology and Transformation of Retail Study

But I honestly don't think there's any other choice than to proactively work toward a higher level of transparency and trust with your customers today and tomorrow.

Let's consider a hypothetical example from another industry that stood is now experiencing disruption:

About ten years ago, I bet there was a convention of taxi-cab company owners, and I'll wager that it was very similar to our NADA convention.

At this event, all the owners and business leaders were standing around with champagne, toasting their ongoing success.

The toasts included "We have a monopoly and a license to print money" and "we're regulated in some cities and besides, who's going to go out and buy billions worth of cabs to compete with us?"

Except Uber didn't get the memo.

And within a few years, the same taxi industry leaders who were toasting their success were licking their wounds.

In Q1 2014, ride-hailing was a mere 8 percent of the business traveler ground transportation market, while rental cars were 55 percent and taxis were 37 percent.

By Q1 2018, ride-hailing had grabbed 70.5 percent of the market, with rental cars getting 23.5 percent and taxis just 6 percent.[*] New York taxi medallions, worth a million dollars as recently as 2014, are now worth $170,000[**].

Here's the really sobering part – Uber didn't even invent any new technology. They went to the technology shelf and took some mobile, added some GPS and added a little social media and presto – over $50 billion valuation. Uber was founded in March 2009.

Does anyone still believe this level of disruption can't happen in automotive?

It's my hope that dealers recognize the situation we're in and act with urgency.

We just started a new decade, as an industry let's approach it as the "decade of the consumer", change our business practices and embrace new ways to connect with consumers in a more transparent and trusting fashion.

I'm not being dramatic when I say the future depends on it.

Jim Roche, December 20th, 2019